G000025764

MALLOW
NEWS

Fake news and comment from Ireland's favourite
moderately popular Twitter feed @mallownews

MALLOW NEWS

Fake news and comment from Ireland's favourite
moderately popular Twitter feed @mallownews

HACHETTE
BOOKS
IRELAND

Stephen Black, aka @mallownews, is an author and lover from Mallow, the Aleppo of North Cork.

Taking to Twitter five long years ago in an attempt to quieten the voice of desperation that gnaws at his soul, he now spends each day trying to come up with amusing ways of saying all life is pain and death is the only constant.

When he's not screaming into the digital void, he can be found reading a good book or participating in illegal socially distanced cock fights at one of Mallow's many abandoned warehouses.

Illustrator Cathal O'Gara is also a designer, production editor, sub-editor, actor/model/writer/dancer/part-time dandy and occasional good person based in Dublin, Ireland. Raised in Mallow, Co Cork, he needs innumerable jobs to pay for the rising cost of therapy.

Mr O'Gara was born in 1990 and is likely to die in February, 2037 – it's a long story but it basically involves the beheading of a Thomas Davis statue, a Faustian bargain with the Seoige sisters' coven and a childhood dream to become the first male member of The Nolans.

His parents are deeply disappointed in him.

Author acknowledgements

First off, I would like to thank my wife and family for their support, without which the book would definitely not have happened.

Thanks also to Ciara Considine in Hachette Ireland, for her help and guidance in how to write proper.

The illustrations in this book are the excellent work of Cathal O'Gara who has lent an air of authenticity to the, quite frankly, disturbing content.

To the Irish government, thanks for the material.

Finally, to all regular readers – thanks for the retweets but I swear to god, you better fucking buy this book after all the years of free laughs I've given you. I'm serious. And don't wait for the paperback either.

First published in 2020 by Hachette Books Ireland

A CIP catalogue record for this title is available from the British Library.

Mallow News is a satirical Twitter account by Stephen Black. *Mallow News* the book uses invented names in all the stories, except in cases when public figures are being satirised. Any other use of real names is accidental and coincidental.

ISBN 978 1 52934 145 4

Interior and cover design by Cathal O'Gara
Cover images: Pixabay, PA Images, Inpho and Rolling News
Printed and Bound in Slovenia by the GPS Group

Hachette Books Ireland policy is to use papers that are natural, renewable and recyclable products and made from wood grown in sustainable forests. The logging and manufacturing processes are expected to conform to the environmental regulations of the country of origin.

Hachette Books Ireland
8 Castlecourt Centre
Castleknock
Dublin 15, Ireland
A division of Hachette UK Ltd
Carmelite House, 50 Victoria Embankment, EC4Y 0DZ
www.hachettebooksireland.ie

Contents

Introduction by Fr Cannon

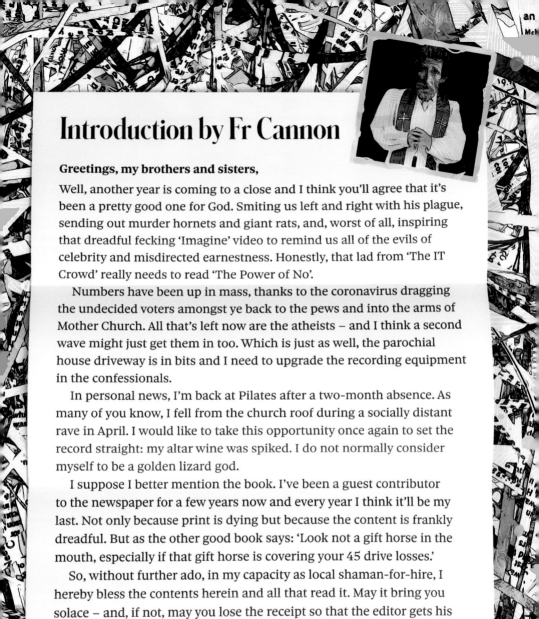

Greetings, my brothers and sisters,

Well, another year is coming to a close and I think you'll agree that it's been a pretty good one for God. Smiting us left and right with his plague, sending out murder hornets and giant rats, and, worst of all, inspiring that dreadful fecking 'Imagine' video to remind us all of the evils of celebrity and misdirected earnestness. Honestly, that lad from 'The IT Crowd' really needs to read 'The Power of No'.

Numbers have been up in mass, thanks to the coronavirus dragging the undecided voters amongst ye back to the pews and into the arms of Mother Church. All that's left now are the atheists – and I think a second wave might just get them in too. Which is just as well, the parochial house driveway is in bits and I need to upgrade the recording equipment in the confessionals.

In personal news, I'm back at Pilates after a two-month absence. As many of you know, I fell from the church roof during a socially distant rave in April. I would like to take this opportunity once again to set the record straight: my altar wine was spiked. I do not normally consider myself to be a golden lizard god.

I suppose I better mention the book. I've been a guest contributor to the newspaper for a few years now and every year I think it'll be my last. Not only because print is dying but because the content is frankly dreadful. But as the other good book says: 'Look not a gift horse in the mouth, especially if that gift horse is covering your 45 drive losses.'

So, without further ado, in my capacity as local shaman-for-hire, I hereby bless the contents herein and all that read it. May it bring you solace – and, if not, may you lose the receipt so that the editor gets his share of the royalties and I stay one week ahead of the loan sharks.

Love in prayer,

Fr Cannon

Local ●NEWS

Drive-by ashing claims another victim

GARDAÍ are investigating this morning after a man was hospitalised when a car carrying two priests pulled up alongside him and opened fire, violently ashing him against his will. Eyewitnesses reported seeing a green Ford Focus fleeing the scene very slowly.

The victim, who is in his twenties, was taken to hospital, where he was treated for mild concussion and irritation. He is expected to make a full recovery but is no longer giving up sweets for Lent.

Authorities have blamed this senseless attack on the notorious Bloodz of Christ gang who are currently engaged in a bitter turf war – with rival gang The Resurrectionists – for parking rights at the local community hall. Sergeant Sam Purvis has appealed to members of both gangs to de-escalate tensions before it's too late. 'It's only a matter of time before someone gets killed,' he said, 'especially given their average age is 84.'

Gardai at Mallow have asked anyone who witnessed this attack or who has information that can assist to contact the station, though not on Thursdays between 5p.m. and 8p.m., as that's movie night.

Man haunted by fellow driver not returning his raised finger salute

A LOCAL man was left distraught yesterday after being involved in a distressing breach of country driving etiquette.

Local father of two Peter Golden was on his way home from work when he spotted a car approaching in the distance. As it came closer, Peter raised his index finger two inches from the steering wheel in strict accordance with the unwritten rules of the road. What happened next appalled him.

'He didn't bother his hole returning the salute!' Peter told *Mallow News*.

'I was so appalled, I nearly drove my Avensis into the ditch.'

Mr Golden was treated at the scene for shock before being taken to Mallow Hospital, where he was administered with a mild sedative and kept overnight for observation.

Speaking from his hospital bed and surrounded by his loving family, Mr Golden was stable but still shaken.

'I mean, did he not see me do it? Was I too subtle? I know some people lift their entire hand off the wheel, but I'm a traditionalist at heart.'

Garda investigators working on the case have gathered CCTV footage from the area and are analysing it for clues to the driver's identity.

'It's early days yet,' said Garda Thomas Foley, 'but we're currently working on the basis that this was a Dublin driver. They're awful animals.'

Whatever the result, it will be some time before Peter Golden gets back behind the wheel of a car. 'He's a changed man,' said his wife Sandra. 'I don't think he'll ever drive again. I'm afraid he'll do something crazy like walk or buy a bicycle.'

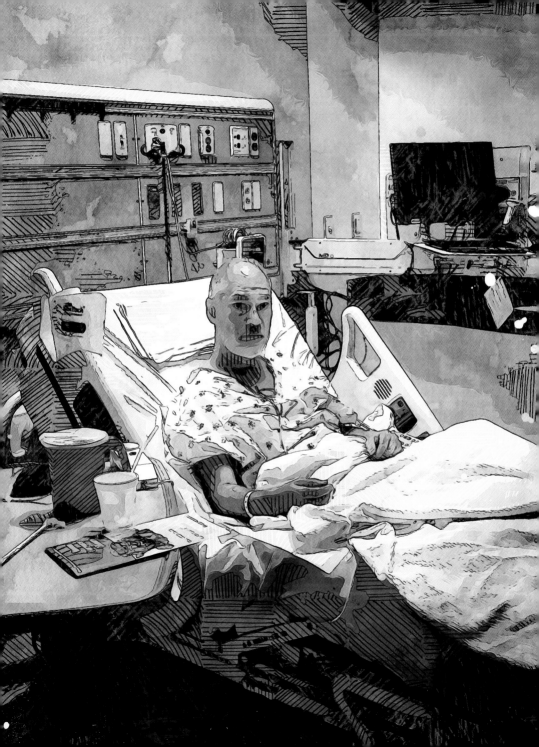

St Anthony arrested after gardaí recover €200,000 worth of stolen goods

A MAN in his late 700s was arrested by gardaí following the discovery of over 200,000 euro worth of stolen goods at his premises in Killavullen today.

The man, identified as one Anthony of Padua, was detained at Mallow garda station under Section 4 of the Criminal Justice Act.

'The suspect was found to be in possession of over 200 grand's worth of single earrings, contact lenses, engagement and wedding rings, even dogs,' said Superintendent Ted Fleming. 'He would steal an item, wait a week and then return to the scene of the crime, pretending that he had just found it "by God's own guidance". Victims would then be pressured into donating.'

It is understood the man, originally from Portugal, had been operating in the area for a few hundred years. Gardaí were alerted to his activities after he attempted to return a set of car keys to an absent-minded local woman for the second time in a week.

He has since been charged and is due to appear before the Central Criminal Court later this month.

The arrest was part of an ongoing investigation under Operation Sacred Heart, targeting so-called saints involved in theft and con artistry. One Jude of James, operating out of Dromahane, was convicted last week of attempting to convince people he could support hopeless causes and was arrested after trying to convince Cork footballers they could make it to Croke Park this year.

Aontú celebrates second Árd Fheis in town phone box

MALLOW was part of history this week as minority party Aontú held their second ever Árd Fheis in the town's last functioning phone box. Irish for 'Continuity Renua', Aontú was formed when leader Peadar Tóibín left Sinn Féin because of his belief that he knows what's best for a woman's body despite having a man's one.

Normally a repository for chicken bones and urine, the phone box was used for similar purposes in 2015 to launch the Social Democrats.

Dressed like a baby applying for a small business loan, Mr Tóibín told *Mallow News* that he was looking forward to giving his address to himself and to discussing his plans for his future. When asked if he would be taking any questions from the floor, he demurred, saying that while he embraced open and democratic dialogue, there wasn't time to hear his other opinions as he was paying by the hour.

He then left quickly, in order to discourage two teenagers from engaging in sexual intercourse on his PA system.

The Aontú Árd Fheis will be streamed live on Aertel this Saturday at 8p.m.

Cork man thinks he's a feminist now

CORK mechanic Dale Fenton declared himself a bona fide feminist yesterday when he let his wife of 15 years have an extra hour's sleep on International Women's Day.

Typically, his wife Coleen could be woken at the crack of dawn by her oldest child Ashton (5) looking for his breakfast while Dale continued to sleep deeply, dreaming of football and gentle misogyny.

Yesterday was different, though. Dale jumped from his bed like a man possessed, bundling all three children downstairs and feeding them bowls of dry cereal before washing them with the power hose in the back garden.

After exactly 60 minutes, he gently woke Coleen and told her lovingly 'not to take the piss' and that he was pretty sure the baby needed changing.

Talking to *Mallow News*, Coleen said she was proud of her husband and hoped this was only the beginning. 'Maybe he'll start ironing or telling me he loves me,' she said.

What motivated Dale's behaviour remains a mystery, although friends say it may have something to do with the attractive new receptionist at work telling him she found considerate men 'really sexy'.

Local school promises to release Senior Infants as soon as voluntary contribution has been paid

A LOCAL primary school has taken its entire Senior Infants class hostage due to what it calls a 'disappointing lack of compliance' with its mandatory voluntary contribution scheme.

Principal of St Agnes School for Boys Karl Utter said the entire situation was 'regrettable' but unavoidable. 'We have given parents every opportunity to comply. We take all major credit cards, bitcoin and, Chinese markets permitting, viable livers and kidneys.'

Incentivisation has also formed an integral part of convincing parents to pay. 'We've included a premium teaching package where students with the highest contributions get access to exclusive educational content, such as the truth about what happened to the five little ducks and the secret twenty-seventh letter of the alphabet.'

Despite this, compliance was only at 25 per cent by September, so a more drastic approach was called for.

'We gathered all the Senior Infants in the assembly hall and told them they wouldn't be able to go home until their parents ponied up.'

Parents who came to collect their children were told they would be released on payment of the outstanding fees. It was a bold move. But will it work?

'I'd have paid them to keep my boy,' said one local parent. 'Myself and the wife are off to west Cork for the weekend on the strength of this. We assume he'll be fine, sure he's with all his friends.

Update: One week later, the school shows no sign of backing down, with the most recent newsletter containing photos of the students being waterboarded with MiWadi.

Young Cork man with hand down trousers confident penis is still there

NINETEEN-YEAR-OLD Cork man Tiernan Savage was happy to confirm yesterday that, after much research, his penis was still in its traditional location, the area commonly known as the 'front-pantal' region.

Tiernan, like many of his peers, spends much of his time ensuring that his penis does not fall prey to the notorious wandering member syndrome, where a man's 'constant companion' just detaches and takes to the road, perhaps solving mysteries or writing the next great Irish novel.

'I like to keep a good grip just in case,' he told *Mallow News*, 'but I got distracted texting my mate Gary and a whole ten minutes had gone without checking. I was bricking it. I heard this lad over in Ballyvolane took his hands off it for only a minute and it had already made it as far as Kent Station and was about to hop on a train to Limerick Junction before he caught up.'

Panicked, Tiernan sent his right hand down hoping that he was still en-penised. 'Luckily, it was still there. From now on I'm texting with one hand only.'

Wandering member syndrome aside, he revealed that it's also important to keep a hand down there in case any members of the opposite sex forget that he is, in fact, the operator of a penis and exclude him from any potential sexual encounters. 'If a beour walks past and I'm not holding my langer then I could be missing out on a ride,' he said, before admitting he had yet to find any evidence to support this theory.

If you or any member of your family has been affected by wandering member syndrome, please call the HSE hotline at 1850-WANDER.

Local teen really wishes parents weren't using lockdown as an opportunity for erotic rediscovery

PÁDRAIG KENNY is finding lockdown particularly difficult. At 17 years of age, he should be busy studying for his state exams. But there's a problem.

'My parents are constantly riding,' he tells *Mallow News* from his home in Churchtown. 'It's non-stop.'

The events in question started one week into lockdown when Pádraig began seeing startling changes in his parents' behaviour. 'They started talking to each other more. Then the scented candles from downstairs disappeared. Dad started playing Bruce Springsteen all the time and Mam took to calling him her "Sexual Joe Wick". Next thing you know, they're spending day and night in their bedroom.'

Soon after, all types of packages were arriving at the front door. 'The only time I'd see them was when the postman arrived. Dad flying downstairs in his kimono to collect the post before I'd get a chance to see what it was. But I've checked their browser history. It's all sex manuals, herbal aids and lubricant.'

At this stage, Pádraig is worried about the effect his parents' new-found erotomania is having on his studies. 'It's hard to concentrate on the *modh coinníollach* when your dad's just sprained his hip from doing a reverse Thai monk bonanza on your mother,' he said. 'I was reading *The Tempest* at dinner last night and she joked that she knew what that felt like. I don't even know what that means.'

Pádraig's parents were sadly unavailable for comment as they had just received a consignment of love masks from southern Indonesia.

Cork man confirms that meaningful conversation with wife no substitute for sport

A WHOLE month of worldwide lockdown has affected us all in many ways, and sports-mad Declan Madden (not his real name) is no exception. Under ordinary circumstances, he'd be spending all his spare time watching football, soccer, hurling, even Azerbaijani goat-throwing. But not anymore.

'It's all reruns now,' he fumes, 'the Coors Lite of sports. About three days into quarantine and I had these mad sweats and headaches. I thought I was infected but when I saw my two kids taking lumps out of each other, the headaches subsided. I knew then what I had to do.'

He spent the rest of the morning making an octagon out of toilet roll holders and sticky tape. 'I was two rounds into an ultimate death match when my wife came in and told me it was "unhealthy" for me to be encouraging my children to choke each other out.'

Things were bad, but they were about to get worse.

'My missus said that this quarantine was a blessing in disguise, that we should use the time "to reconnect", to have a real conversation. Not just me pretending to listen to her shiteing on while I'm glued to the sports.'

All excuses exhausted, he thought he'd give it a try.

'I promised her I'd do my best and listen. I took her hands and looked her straight in the eyes as she told me about her day and how the quarantine was affecting her. I started feeling actual emotions, from a conversation with my wife. That's not normal, like.'

As the minutes passed, however, he found himself in trouble.

'My concentration started to drift. The only way I could keep listening to her work stories was to imagine I was get-

ting a team talk from my favourite football manager, so I just pictured Jürgen Klopp, but with tits.'

Eventually, as the minutes turned into an hour, he got through it. And the results of this face off?

'She thinks this has been a total success and we've had a "breakthrough". I don't have the heart to tell her all it's done is give me very complicated feelings about Jürgen Klopp. She expects us to talk every day now. What if she starts asking me questions? I'll be fucked.'

If you have been affected by any of the topics covered in this column, please remember that all sport is pointless and any search for vicarious success through the achievements of others is only a distraction from our inexorable advance towards the endless abyss of death.

BUSINESS

Local man bows out on Dragons' Den

DARRAGH BUSWELL, primary-school teacher and traditional musician, thought he had the perfect business idea – all he needed was the proper investment. An appearance on *Dragons' Den*, RTÉ's show for budding entrepreneurs with no sense of self-awareness, seemed like the right move.

'I went into the room with my head high,' he tells *Mallow News* from his home in Ballyclough. 'I explained the concept: a mobile-phone app that would help teach children how to play traditional Irish music on the violin. They were hooked immediately. One of them offered me €10,000 straightaway if I could guarantee only red-haired colleens with MAGA hats could use it. I had them all in the palm of my hand. Then, they asked me what the name of the app was.'

It was at that moment his fortunes took a turn for the worse.

'When I told them it was called Kiddie Fiddler, suddenly the room went quiet. Gavin Duffy asked if it was a wind-up.

I said no, it was a traditional fiddle. Then, he suggested I change the name and that's when I left. I mean, you either believe in yourself or you don't. I'm not selling my dream for 30 pieces of silver.'

In retrospect, maybe he could have changed the name?

'I don't see what the issue is. It's built for kids and it teaches them how to fiddle. Plus, it's a name you easily remember.'

It's not all bad news, though.

'Whenever one door closes, another opens. A consortium of investors from the Catholic Church got in touch after the episode aired and said they were very interested. I was delighted. I told them that with the money they were offering, I could upload regular videos dedicated to fingering techniques. They almost passed out.'

Kiddie Fiddler will be available to buy for Apple and Android phones in late 2020. Since the interview, Darragh has vacated his position at Scoil Madrigal.

Heartbreak as Mallow eliminated from Tidy Towns competition for fourth year running

'A LANDFILL, only less sentient' was how Tidy Town judges described Mallow in their most recent report, explaining why our beloved town was once again eliminated from this superficial beauty pageant. The report, which was incomplete due to two members of the panel being hospitalised with dengue fever, also stated that, from now on, Mallow would have to be assessed remotely, via drone.

Tony Pedant, chair of the local Tidy Towns committee, resigned soon after the report was released. 'This isn't my fault,' he said.

'It's this fucking town. There's more community spirit in a mass grave. The judging panel found a dissected giraffe corpse in the playground, for Christ's sake. The nearest zoo is 45 miles away. Every year, we ask people to just try to be tidier, just for a month – that's all – and every year they redouble their efforts to be even filthier. I heard a rumour on WhatsApp that one fella shipped in a tonne of dog shite especially from Carraig na Bhfear and dumped it in the swimming pool. Parents deliberately dress their kids in flour sacks and send them wandering the streets barefoot eating garbage from the bins like feral cats. It's like *Lord of the Flies* meets *Angela's Ashes*.'

Mallow News talked to Pat (not his real name) of the so-called Anti-Tidy Towns Militia and asked him why local resistance to the competition was so fierce.

'It's our democratic right to be filthy,' he said, throwing a half-eaten snack box into oncoming traffic. 'A clean Mallow is no Mallow at all. It's like putting

concealer on a leper. Our town charter was originally written in badger entrails and was thrown into the local well afterwards, where it gave the townsfolk chronic diarrhoea for months. That's our heritage, that's what these litter Nazis want to take away from us – well, I for one am not having it.'

What if they insist on applying next year?

'We have contingencies in place. I know a lad in Wuhan who has a rake of bat meat he can't get rid of.'

Mallow Tidy Towns Committee will convene next week; applications are invited for chairperson.

UNESCO upgrades Buttevant from slum to shantytown

UNESCO has declared that north Cork pimple Buttevant is to lose its slum status and will now be officially designated a shantytown. The decision comes following a surprise audit conducted by official inspectors last month. The auditors recommended the upgrade due to the recent eradication of malaria in the area, a result of direct intervention by the Global Billionaire Guilt Assuagement Initiative last autumn.

Buttevant town mayor Gordon Tuohy spoke of his disappointment at the recommendations. 'When they sent me a copy of the report I was disgusted, as they know I can't read. There's a doctor that comes down from Dublin every month to conduct tests on us, so I asked him to read it to me. When he did, I tell you I was so shocked, my hair fell out! Though the doctor says that's probably due to the 18 different types of medicines he has me on.'

A lack of consultation has also added to local hurt and confusion. 'They never even discussed it with me before making their decision. Apparently "direct contact with primitive beings" is against their Prime Directive or something. It's plain as the nose on my face that this is a slum. The corrugated roofing, the body of water flowing through our open sewers, the dead eyes of our children as they face another day. That all screams "slum" to me. But no, you let Bill feckin' Gates test a vaccine on you and suddenly you're a shantytown.'

The mayor now fears the kind of gentrification that normally follows this kind of reclassification. 'There'll be running water, I suppose, people will want their rat cooked instead of raw. Expectations will be different. The smallies will want to work making fancy runners for Nike

instead of going down the salt mines. Christ, some of them might even want to go to secondary school.'

Ironically, stepping up in class will have a direct impact on potential investments. 'The lads who make that *Walking Dead* show on the telly have said they were interested in filming down here – said they'd save a fortune on makeup and set design. Can't see them wanting to film in a shantytown, they'll probably feck off to Kanturk or England.'

Mallow News did invite UNESCO to respond to this piece but was told they 'couldn't be arsed'.

Rogue 'Siege of Ennis' maims four

IT WAS mayhem on the dancefloor at the Majestic Ballroom yesterday after four people were hospitalised when a 'Siege of Ennis'* went horribly wrong.

Emergency services attended the scene, where tourists had gathered to watch local dance troupe the Dead Legs Céilí Crew perform. Four of the dancers were taken to Mallow General, where they remain stable after a number of surgical procedures.

Mallow News understands the incident occurred when the crew attempted to augment their performance with a forbidden dance move – the Cromwell Manoeuvre – much to the delight of onlookers.

Joy quickly turned to horror, however, as the measured movements of the dancers became less controlled and more frenzied. According to eyewitnesses, lead dancer Jim Flange ended with his foot up his own anus, while Gearóid Teehan was blinded by his own elbow.

Twin sisters Ailish and Aisling O'Connor were more fortunate, even if they had to get their stomachs pumped so surgeons could retrieve their severed toes for reattachment.

Several tourists who fell in the ensuing blood slick were treated for superficial injuries at the scene.

'It's incredibly difficult and totally banned by the union,' said traditional-dance expert Ceoltas Bannon. 'It has only ever been performed on the céilí underground. Michael Flatley attempted it in a Hanoi dance pit in 2002 and ended up with a punctured lung. I am horrified that anyone would try it here in Ireland.'

While the gardaí will not be pressing any charges, the consequences for the Dead Legs Céilí Crew will still be severe. 'They'll never be able to dance again,' said Mr Bannon. 'There's no rhythm in guilty feet.'

The 'Siege of Ennis' was a dance invented in 1801 by the Catholic Church to replace foreplay.

Local man walking ahead of his dog doing a shit – that surprised face isn't fooling anyone, reports Shane Collins

DARREN SCALLY, local dose and well-known hypocrite, takes his labradoodle Alfie for a walk in the park every morning before going to work. Blithely ignoring the 'All dogs must be on a leash' sign, because he knows that only applies to other people, Darren strolls around checking his work emails and listening to a Joe Rogan podcast while Alfie trots faithfully behind him. When nature eventually takes its course, Darren is confident that he has built up significant distance between him and his dog to claim plausible deniability should the worst happen, and another dog walker asks him to pick up his own dog's shit.

Even in this scenario, Darren is prepared. Putting on a shocked yet slightly put-out face, he will thank the stranger and produce a poo bag to show his willingness to comply. He will then engage in a grotesque pantomime where he will slowly probe the grass with his feet like a human mine detector, occasionally throwing his arms out in mock frustration. This act will last about five minutes, by which stage his accuser will have either walked on or given up. Darren will then give himself a mental high five and continue his walk, happy in the knowledge that he's beaten the system, although he's just a selfish prick.

INTERVIEW

Life after politics:
Joan Burton finds purpose in new role

ON A ROCK by a cliff overlooking the River Blackwater, former Minister for Social Protection Joan Burton sits, combing her hair with a magpie's beak and reflecting on her life in politics.

'I was a TD for almost 30 years,' she says. 'I knew nothing else but the cut and thrust of politics. I never dreamed I would find a second purpose in life.'

For the past two months, Joan has served as Mallow's official banshee-in-residence. A shrieking harbinger of doom, Ms Burton was a natural fit for the job, or so you would think.

'I was afraid of being typecast but once Trevor (Foley, lord mayor) told me the pay and conditions, I couldn't say no.'

Being a banshee is a serious business and Joan brings the same passion she displayed in her Oireachtas days to her new role.

'Firstly, there's the wailing,' she laughs. 'I mean, we can agree I have that down. Maintaining an air of misery at all times. It's the role I was born to play. It can be hard on the throat, though, so I make sure I always have my Strepsils at hand. And water … it's important to stay hydrated when you're crying all the time.'

It's not all positives, though.

'Ultimately, I am warning people that a member of their household is going to die, which is fine, but they can get quite annoyed if I interrupt *Gogglebox* or scare the cattle.'

The job provides permanent accommodation, a fairy mound or sidhe which forms Joan's main base of operations.

'It's damp but the broadband's actually quite good and the rent is reasonable.'

Loneliness can be a factor as locals can be quite superstitious.

'They cross the street when they see me,' she admits, 'but that used to happen in the Dáil as well, so it's not a big deal.'

As she packs up for a night's work, Joan wants to make it clear that she takes nothing for granted.

'There's a lot of competition out there – RIP.ie for one – but I don't think that will ever replace the personal touch that I bring. After all, there's something comforting about being alerted to the death of a loved one by seeing a former minister flying past your window howling dementedly. That's something no website or app can give you.'

Interview ended, she floats ethereally through the trees and is gone. For now.

Local woman arrested for selling Daniel O'Donnell's bedsheets on dark web

MARGARET ROBINSON, a resident of Mallow town and popular hostess of BR Guest House, was arrested by members of the Garda National Cyber Crime Bureau for attempting to sell what she claimed to be the used bed linen of Irish country-music legend Daniel O'Donnell on the internet.

Ms Robinson participated in the popular RTÉ show *Daniel and Majella's B&B Road Trip,* where the celebrity couple travel the towns and villages of Ireland while staying in B&B accommodation. They spent one night in Robinson's guest house while taking in Mallow's finest sights – the castle, the leper colony in Bweeng and the magic hill where cars stop for no reason. As soon as they left, with nothing but fond memories and potentially some leprosy, their host sprang into action, stripping the bed – and her reputation – in what she later admitted to

detectives was 'a moment of madness'.

A post on fandannyboy.org appeared soon after, advertising the sheets as a genuine relic of St Daniel O'Donnell with tasting notes describing them as having the primary aromas of 'Rich Tea and Old Spice'. The asking price was a startling one thousand euro.

Luckily, gardaí received an anonymous tip and sprang into action, raiding Ms Robinson's home in the early hours of Friday morning. But for what crime, exactly?

'It's actually illegal in Ireland to sell the bedclothes or bath water of a public figure,' explains Sergeant Tom Maguire. 'Charlie Haughey got the legislation in the back door in the eighties while he was doing a line with yer wan from the *Independent.* I think Fine Gael had got hold of a soiled kimono and were threatening to expose him if he didn't resign.'

And is this a regular occurrence?

'Sadly, yes. Most of the people participating in the show are lovely but there are a few genuine perverts who use the opportunity to make a quick buck. There was a lady in Galway who set up a webcam in the jacks and was trying to sell explicit footage of wee Daniel's wee Daniel before we managed to intervene and shut down the auction. The bidding had just got to over a thousand euro as well. Bedsheets are particularly valuable among the more rabid fans as they are believed to heal ailments such as arthritis, rheumatism and chronic loneliness. Some see it as an opportunity to perhaps clone their own Daniel – as soon as science catches up, that is.'

When asked by *Mallow News* if there was any truth to the rumour that Majella and Daniel's travel itinerary mirrored a string of nationwide missing-person cases, Sergeant Maguire declined to comment.

Public warning:
Ross activity on the rise

MEMBERS of the public have been asked to remain vigilant after an increase in the number of Shane Ross sightings in the north Cork area earlier this week. The former Minister for Sport has been roaming the country since losing his seat in 2020, turning up at random events and attempting to take credit for them.

Gardaí are advising people to keep their distance and, if approached, to just give him the selfie. 'That's all he wants – for God's sake don't feed him.'

Unfortunately, this warning comes too late for a couple of unlucky locals.

Blushing groom Niall Mackey was enjoying the fruits of his marriage bed with his new bride Mary Murphy when, all of a sudden, the former minister appeared. 'It took me a second before it registered who he was,' said a visibly shaken Mr Mackey. 'He pulled me off Mary and took a quick selfie, before clicking his heels three times and jumping out the window.'

'He seemed nice enough,' said Mrs Murphy. 'Although I've no idea how he got in. We locked the door behind us. He must have been under the bed for hours.'

Local mother of two Karen Bailey was just about to bury her mother when she heard a knocking noise from inside the coffin. 'I thought the hospital had made a terrible mistake but when they opened it up that feckin' eejit Shane Ross jumped out, screamed, "This is for my K-pop stans" and made a TikTok of himself flossing on the corpse. One of the gravediggers had to put the hose on him to get him to leave.'

While no one has been hurt, victims are describing the experience as 'irritating' and 'unnecessary'. Official guidelines for dealing with Mr Ross are available from the HSE website and the DSPCA.

Ticket-vending machine wins Irish Rail Employee of the Year

MALLOW Station was the scene of jubilant celebration this week as Ticket Vending Machine Serial No. XcH2001 (nicknamed 'That fecking lick' by its colleagues) was given the coveted Irish Rail Employee of the Year Award for 2020.

According to company policy, this award recognises 'outstanding achievements in the field of customer service, going above and beyond the call of duty by actually providing Irish Rail customers with a positive experience'. Specifically, XcH2001 was cited for 'working properly, dispensing tickets when required and being compatible with all major credit cards'.

Accepting the award and prize mon-ey on the machine's behalf was Lord Mayor Alan 'The Abattoir' Conroy. 'This machine is a model employee who has only had one day off in the last two years, and that was after Dan Foley gawked up a scampi box all over the touch-screen and an IT lad from Cork had to come down and fix it. We use the word "hero" too lightly these days but I think it's safe to say XcH2001 is the greatest hero who's ever lived or at least that's been mass manufactured in a plant in South Korea.'

When asked by a reporter if it was unusual for an inanimate object to win an award like this, Mayor Alan said, 'No, a driver from Limerick Junction won it last year.'

Literary

CORNER

Exclusive extract from latest JCWACG book Part 1

MALLOW NEWS Literary Corner is delighted to bring you this teaser from the upcoming third book in the 'Jesus Christ What A Complete Gobnait' series, A *Tale of Two Gobnaits*, which continues the trials and tribulations of human resources admin Gobnait McSweeney as she navigates the world of romance and friendship in a way that exploits that strange Irish tendency to latch on to nostalgia like a teat that dispenses morphine. Anyway, enjoy.

I love Cork city to my bones, I don't care who knows it. Blackpool, the English Market, drisheen. The way the light hits the faces of the homeless lads drinking cans on the benches of Bishop Lucey Park. Pure joy.

'What the fuck are you staring at?' says one of them, staggering in my direction. I hurry past, high heels clacking on my way to the office, making sure not to make eye contact with his you-know-what which he has just taken out and is swinging like a compass needle in the Bermuda Triangle. Good girls don't look, not even with their boyfriend.

I've been doing a line with Gary Barry for four months now and I've never ever seen his Shandon bells, preferring instead the comfort of the darkened room and an approach to lovemaking that could only be described as 'erotic Braille'. Gary was grand about it, though. He's a chartered accountant in his early thirties, so he could wait a little longer before seeing a woman naked.

I arrive at the office half an hour early as always and set about my day in a way that is vaguely relatable to some girl you

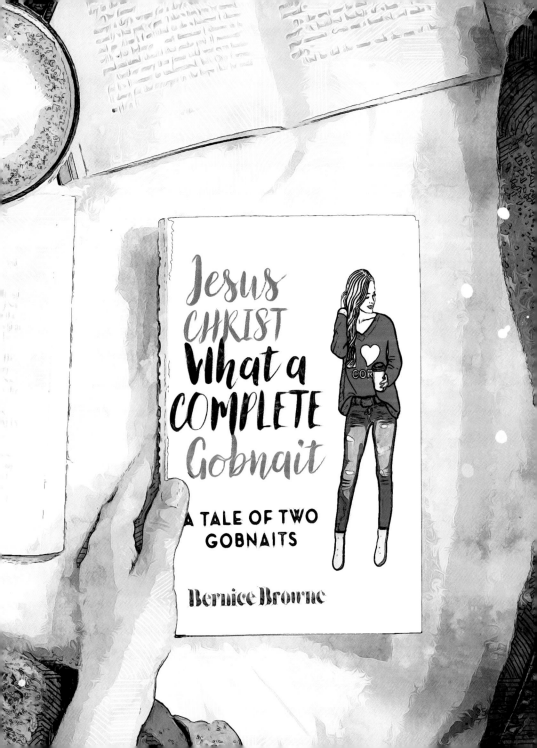

know, used to know or, even better, is you. Great stuff, keep reading – we might get a TV series out of this next.

Tina, the other girl who works in the office, is chattering away.

'Oh my weekend was just nuts,' she says.

Tina is a real wild card but also has a heart of gold, like myself, because you don't want to alienate readers by being 100 per cent a gowl, like.

'How so?' I say, absentmindedly sending a WhatsApp to Gary reminding him to turn off the immersion.

'Well, I met this fella in a pub that readers will be familiar enough with, then we hit a club that has similar nostalgic vibes … next thing you know, I'm being auctioned to a room of oligarchs in a shipping container down the docks.'

'Jesus, Tina,' I say. 'Not again.'

'I know, I know, fool me once. Anyway, lucky for me the guards raided the place just as the bidding reached ten grand.'

'Oh that's much better than last time,' I exclaimed.

A girl should always value herself but it's nice for a little external validation now and then, even if it is from some lad with a teardrop tattoo and cologne that smells like a St Petersburg brothel.

'What happened last time?'

We both turn, mouths open, to see this fella stood in the doorway with a cheeky grin on his face. Dressed really nice, like the upstairs of a Topman, handsome with golden hair the colour of flat Tanora.

'Who are you?' says Tina, discreetly undoing the top button of her blouse because, as we've established, she's a stereotypical sexually aggressive tart.

'I'm Tom. Tom Lyons, the new assistant manager.'

He stares at me and I swear to God my stomach leaps like it's one in the morning and I'm about to destroy a Hillbilly's snackbox.

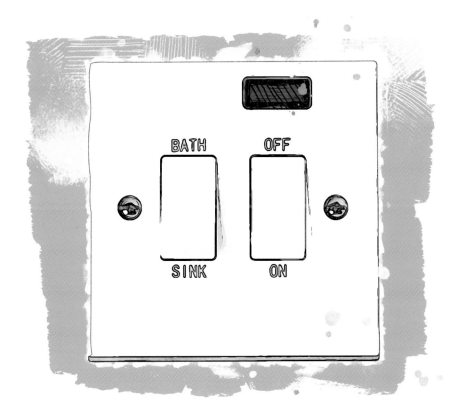

'Who are you?' he purrs. He has the physique of a Na Piarsaigh full-back who's been mainlining protein shakes like a secondary-school teacher doing shots at an open bar.

'Go—' I stutter.

'Go?' he mocks gently. 'But I only just got here.'

Tina lets a screech out of her like a goat about to be eaten by a T-Rex. 'You're gaaaas,' she gushes.

Gathering myself, I say, 'Gobnait. My name's Gobnait. And this harpie is Tina.

I suppose you're looking for your ID card and a tour of the building?'

'That'd be sound out. May I?' he says, extending his arm.

My heart quickens as I unwrap his laminate and take his arm. Just as we're about to leave, I get a text back from Gary: *What immersion? We have a combi boiler, you mentalist.*

Will Gobnait be a good Cork girl and choose Barry over Lyons? Find out in *A Tale of Two Gobnaits*, available soon in all good bookstores.

Horoscopes

WITH TINA PENDRAGON

WHAT mysteries do the stars hold for you? Let Tina Pendragon, astrologer and chartered accountant, pierce the bubble of beyond with her needle of foresight. Remember, this is an exact science, as proved recently by scientists at MIT (Mallow Institute of Technology).

Aries
You will spend time screaming internally at an elderly woman slowly counting her change at the tills in Tesco. The smell of paprika will influence a financial investment.

Taurus
One of your children will join Young Fine Gael. You already suspect which one. You will be tempted to go to Dublin, thinking it can't be as bad as you remember. It is.

Gemini
Stay away from office parties if you want your marriage to remain intact, especially if your name is Derek.

Cancer
You will find a lump in the shower as your ex returns unexpectedly.

Leo
Local radio brings back painful memories. You make an off-colour joke at work that causes your colleagues to think less of you. Travel beckons after receipt of a court summons.

Virgo

It's time to let love in and take a chance on that married astrologer you've been treating for sciatica this past month.

Libra

The time has come to realise relationships are not for you. Invest heavily in cats. You will become tired of people trying to put you in a box and will eventually consent to being buried alive.

Scorpio

You remain overly invested in the lives of Harry and Meghan while resolutely ignoring your own problems. You become convinced you can carry off dreads despite being a middle-class white woman.

Sagittarius

You probably shouldn't listen to the voice in your head urging you to 'kill again' but, admit it, it's the most fun you've ever had. A trip to the Wicklow Mountains brings new opportunities.

Capricorn

You will buy a can of Lilt for some strange nostalgic reason and spend the next week trying to get the totally tropical taste out of your mouth.

Aquarius

You worry about not spending enough time with your children. That's not going to be a problem.

Pisces

You decide to become more adventurous in the bedroom and paint the walls magnolia. You will go to the supermarket then forget entirely why you went there in the first place.

Coddle is an acquired taste, like Simon Coveney or Protestants, but once you get past the initial retching, you'll wonder how you ever lived without it.
Love, Cathy

Cookery corner
with Cathy

CODDLE

Ingredients
- 1 lb sausages
- 1 lb rashers
- 1 tsp mixed herbs
- 2 tbs barley
- 5 large potatoes
- 1 large onion

I OPENED my kitchen window the other day and the wonderful waft of fresh silage hit my nose, reminding me of my wedding day and this marvellous recipe for coddle, which I'll now share with all of you as part of our continuing series of Irish Culinary Treasures.

Coddle originated in Dublin and comes from the Old Irish *caedal*, which means 'practical joke'. The meal was initially created from the scraps of food the British would throw at Dubliners while they danced for their suppers in the porter fields of Clondalkin. It is thought to have marvellous restorative properties, and Dublin footballers cred-it their recent five-in-a-row success to regular bowls of coddle and 15 million euro in funding from the GAA.

Method

Firstly, roughly chop the onion. Take two of the largest pieces and stuff them in your nostrils. This will help with the smell. Peel the potatoes and wash their naked bodies under the tap while saying a decade of the rosary. Fry the sausages in a pan for a few minutes – remember, you really need to use poor-quality sausages, otherwise you're in danger of adding flavour to a dish that should never have it. Then, take all your ingredients and, without making eye contact, dispose of them in a pot. Cover with water, bring to the boil and simmer. After 45 minutes, or when the first suicidal crow hits your kitchen window, remove from the heat.

Serving suggestion

It has been said that coddle looks like a bunch of old men wrestling naked in a stream. I usually turn the sacred heart to face the wall and cover my head with a tea towel to hide my shame from God, then ladle a helping into a nice tureen. Add salt to taste.

National NEWS

Going, going, gong – RTÉ announces latest cutback

IT WAS a case of 'You've Lost That Loving Pealing' this week when RTÉ director general Dee Forbes announced that the popular religious programme *The Angelus* was to be reduced from 18 rings to one. This was the latest in a series of cost-cutting measures which include minimal pay cuts for high-profile presenters, replacing *Fair City* cast members with barnyard animals and turning off Bosco's life-support system.

The Angelus has been broadcast since 1950 on both radio and television and is perhaps best known for its latter incarnation. Originally showing typical Catholic imagery, such as a priest giving communion or chasing a small child, these days it contains more benign spiritual imagery, such as people gardening, washing their hands or the pope denying redress to the victims of clerical sex abuse.

The original bells were recorded by Beatles' producer George Martin on the grounds of St Mary's Pro-Cathedral and cost the licence-payer approximately 1.5 million euro a year in residuals to his estate. The new recording will consist of Marty Whelan shouting 'BONG' into an iPhone and will cost the licence-payer nothing as, according to an RTÉ accountant, 'We own him, balls and all.'

The move is set to disappoint many people, especially the elderly, who use this time to reflect on God's great glory and as a reminder to take their blood thinners. The Archbishop of Dublin said it was 'disappointing' but that he hoped the people of Ireland would 'bong along at home themselves'.

The Angelus

...of the Lord declared unto Mary,
she conceived of the Holy Spirit

(Hail Mary... the Lord.
...to thy word.

...hold the ha... ...e flesh.
...it done unt... ...ng us.

And th... ...us.
R... ...)

Mother of G...
...e made wort...
Pray... ...ises of Christ
R. Th... forth, we bes...
...r hea...

45

Government puts halt to stag nation: Temple Bar closes in bid to stop spread of unwanted foreign bodies and COVID-19

DUBLIN – Gutters that traditionally ran with piss and vomit today filled with tears and some vomit after the government instructed traders in the Temple Bar area of Dublin to close their doors. This action was taken as a result of stag and hen parties failing to comply with social distancing requirements, and continuing to gather in large groups to drink overpriced Guinness and sing 'Sweet Caroline', like the last days of Sodom sponsored by Lynx Africa and fake tan.

Stunned revellers were seen wandering the cobbled streets, inflatable penises at half mast, unable to think of an alternative to getting absolutely blitzed out of their skulls. One man, dressed as an Oompa Loompa, sat sadly on the kerb, cradling an empty bottle of Jägermeister and gently wailing 'Wonderwall'. Nearby, a group of Liverpudlian nurses tried desperately to stop their hen from garrotting herself with an L plate necklace.

Mallow News spoke to one man who said it was 'a disgrace' and that it was 'bad enough you Paddies don't take sterling, now we can't even have the craic'. Asking that he be called 'Lord of the Bantz', despite one of his friends calling him Colin, he pointed out that the coronavirus only affected the elderly and that his government was going to murder them anyway, so 'What's the point?' When our reporter asked what he did for a living, he proudly replied, 'Care worker.'

Originally created as a refugee camp for morons, Temple Bar has successfully contained the worst elements of Irish tourism, keeping them the fuck out of Cork for years. Some worry this closure may cause the contagion to spread, but it is hoped they'll take the hint instead and piss off back home before Monday.

Taoiseach: 'We're in this together, except for you, you and ... eh ... you as well'

LEO VARADKAR, caretaker Taoiseach and the only man rejected by Scientology, today qualified that his statement regarding the country being in this current crisis together was directed specifically at Fine Gael voters and middle-class golfers.

'It has come to my attention that many of you misunderstood me and thought this was a clarion call for unity during a period of unprecedented strife. This is not the case. When I said "we", I meant me and anyone who votes for the party or thinks singing "Ireland's Call" is the same as donating money to charity. I most certainly did not mean working-class people, Sinn Féin voters or people working in the, God help me, "arts".'

Mr Varadkar once again took the opportunity to target those claiming the 350-euro Pandemic Unemployment Payment, accusing them of exploiting the system, saying there was 'no such thing' as free money.

'This allowance was not brought in to make things better for the poor. The only people who should be benefiting from this crisis are the owners of private hospitals and politicians who technically shouldn't even still be in government.'

The Taoiseach declined to criticise mass gatherings as he was too busy rubbing tanning lotion on his glistening torso.

'Oh, are you lot still here? Sorry. Eh, just insert your own inane pop-culture quote and I'll see you all next Friday.'

The government has recently moved into Phase 1, which allowed for the reopening of garden centres and the passive-aggressive targeting of low-income families for 'gaming the system'.

If infection rates continue to decline, Phase 2 can be initiated, meaning vulnerable workers can be forced back into the workplace and conveniently scapegoated for any future outbreaks.

RIP.ie goes up behind paywall

'More like RIPOFF.IE'
@joedolanfan1102

'Is this how I leave a comment?'
@padrepio69

'This is another deathblow for rural Ireland'
@MHrae

DEATH site RIP.IE will start charging for its content from next Monday under a new pay-as-you-go model, reports our tech correspondent, Mary Finntery.

The site announced today it will charge up to 20 euro a month for its 'premium' digital subscription, while the regular offer starts at 12 euro a month. Premium members will be able to access exclusive new content, such as live streaming of removals and a popularity rating system for the deceased, allowing politicians to make informed decisions regarding which funerals to haunt for votes.

This news left many users furious, turning to the site's message board to vent their anger.

Described as 'PornHub for the over sixties', the site is used primarily for curious aul' wans wanting to know why Bridie's milk has been piling up on her doorstep or for aul' fellas looking to pay their respects while loading up on free triangular sandwiches.

While it is expected most regular users will subscribe, industry experts anticipate a spike in traffic for rival site Dust2Dust.org as a result of the change.

Government partners with Ikea to develop stackable millennials

MINISTER for Business, Enterprise and Innovation Heather Humphreys today announced a new initiative with Swedish furniture manufacturer and divorce specialists Ikea to help tackle Ireland's spiralling rent crisis.

Working closely with the Department of Housing, the aim is to deliver stackable millennials by the year 2025 to enable affordable housing to be delivered more efficiently.

Ikea's scientific advisor Professor Karl Blåg told reporters they had already made 'significant' headway on merging human flesh with MDF and that their new Fükd range would revolutionise how millennials would co-share in the near future.

'Just picture it,' he said via video link from Älmhult in Sweden. 'After a hard day of semi-permanent employment, a millennial can return to his or her home, eat their instant noodle and just collapse into a perfect, aesthetically pleasing cube, powered by the cold-blue glow of their smartphone.' Future phases are aimed at the elimination of toilet rooms by having young people produce cube-shaped poops that will be practically odourless and recyclable.

Minister for Housing Eoghan Murphy said this approach would allow for a more communal experience as up to 50 millennials will be able to fit in a standard two-bed apartment, rather than the current thirty.

'It's so European,' he gushed, 'by which I mean the bleak dystopian body horror produced by Czechoslovakian film-makers in the eighties. We will be providing more space without having to compromise on rent. It won't be long until the entire generation is Fükd.'

Tenants' advocacy groups called the news 'bleak' yet 'inevitable'. Landlords' associations were unavailable for comment as they were too busy tying widows to railway tracks and twirling their moustaches.

Taoiseach closes strategic communications unit in favour of new enchanted mirror

LEO VARADKAR today closed the controversial Strategic Communications Unit (SCU) that has beleaguered his government during his tenure as Taoiseach. Established in 2018, with annual running costs of 5 million euro, the unit's main remit was to modernise and streamline government communications by scripting inspiring speeches for Mr Varadkar that sounded like they came from the bin outside *The West Wing's* writers' room. The unit was also behind many successful public information campaigns such as 'Does Your Granny Need That House?' and 'Welfare Cheats: Subhuman Scum'.

The Taoiseach announced the unit was being wound down in favour of a new enchanted mirror he had received as a gift from an evil queen.

'Joan Burton offered it to me as a parting gift when she retired,' he told *Mallow News*. 'It performs the same function as the SCU, but at a fraction of the cost.'

He then went on to say that the mirror was able to tell him with unwavering honesty that he was the fairest of them all – including Justin Trudeau – and that this, ultimately, is all he ever wanted.

'When I look in the mirror it is able to say, "Leo, you are amazing, you deserve this." I couldn't even get John Concannon to do that. He kept breaking his hole laughing.'

Opposition parties have welcomed the move, acknowledging it was 'weird as all balls' but preferable to the spin generated by the SCU.

Update: Unfortunately, it was seven years' bad luck for the Taoiseach as the mirror has recently started telling him Mary Lou McDonald is the fairest of them all. Witnesses heard the mirror scream 'Up the RA!' before being thrown out a window.

Fine Gael and Fianna Fáil form historic coalition. Again.

IT WAS an end to Civil War politics, dating as far back as January this year, as Fianna Fáil and Fine Gael finally put months of enmity behind them to create a Grand Coalition government.

Uniting under the banner Profits Before People, the new coalition today released a ten-point policy document that had all the focus and coherence of a drunkard shopping for presents on Christmas Eve five minutes before closing time.

'This is a chance for a new government with a new face,' said TD of 30 years Micheál Martin. 'I'm delighted to continue our proud party tradition of fucking the electorate over with one hand and feeding property developers and bankers with the other.'

His new partner was in agreement. 'With this ten-point plan, we've really put previous policies such as our five-point plan in the shade,' said Fine Gael party leader and emotionally dead cyborg Leo Varadkar. 'We're literally twice as good.'

It is understood that the role of Taoiseach will be rotating, like a political rotisserie chicken.

'I don't care who gets it as long as I get it,' said the selfless Mr Martin.

Responding to questions regarding potential unrest in their respective parliamentary parties, the leaders stated that 'all opinions would be welcome' but that everyone needed to pull together for the good of the nation – shorthand for 'they'll do as they're fucking told if they know what's good for them'.

The finer parts of the marriage agreed, it is now a matter of finding a minor party to complete this unholy *ménage à trois*. At present, the Green Party are favourites, as Eamon Ryan is already practically naked, in the hot tub and horsing poppers into himself.

55

Cthulhu calls on Fine Gael parliamentary party to accept new Programme for Government

DEAD-EYED soul stealer and devourer of worlds Leo Varadkar was overjoyed yesterday when his campaign for government received a surprise celebrity endorsement from elder god and multidimensional property developer Cthulhu.

The dark lord will participate in a livestream webinar tomorrow evening to discuss converting soul matter to dark energy, co-living solutions for the modern era and other aspects of the new Programme for Government.

Cthulhu is a long-term supporter of the party, making significant financial contributions over the years, but this is his first public intervention since acting as an advisor during the 1930s.

Speaking to *Mallow News* ahead of the event, he said, 'Being a creature of unfathomable evil and destruction, I have a natural affinity with Fine Gael and have watched with particular interest their capacity for rapacious wantonness grow over the past seven years. This Pro-

gramme for Government offers an opportunity for their evil works to continue and feed my unquenchable thirst for human misery.'

Self-quarantining at his home in the pit of despair, just outside Longford, he noted that he felt compelled to speak out when he saw Hollywood actor Mark Ruffalo address the Green Party. 'Mark and I have a lot in common, we're both surrounded by monsters on a daily basis.'

When asked if he would address the Fianna Fáil parliamentary party, Cthulhu remarked, 'I may be evil incarnate, but I have fucking standards.'

Fianna Fáil 'looking forward' to reminding electorate why they shouldn't have voted for them again

AS THE new Programme for Government was agreed yesterday, rotating-Taoiseach-in-waiting Micheál Martin told assembled journalists that he was looking forward to reminding voters why they stopped voting Fianna Fáil in the first place.

'This is a very exciting time for me, obviously,' he said, smiling like a clown luring a child into a sewer. 'I've been waiting years to lead the country into another recession and finally the time has come. I'd personally like to take this opportunity to thank the Irish electorate's lack of imagination and general dementia, which has resulted in our re-

turn to government only 12 years after we buggered the economy like it was Ned Beatty in *Deliverance*.'

Representatives of Ireland's millennials were also enthusiastic about this return to the old days. 'Nostalgia is our thing, yeah?' said Aoife Colcannon from We Are So Fucking Tired, a generational lobby group that uses memes to treat depression.

'So, it's great to be back under the yoke of one of the worst parties in modern history. I mean, Micheál Martin was in the last government that destroyed our chances of happiness and now he's back for a second crack of the whip. Lol, 🏠 #JesusfuckingChrist.'

The Programme for Government now needs to be ratified by the respective parliamentary parties before the Dáil reconvenes on 26 June, but Mr Martin is confident that his party will row in behind him, if only to get a good clear shot at his back.

Fianna Fáil and Fine Gael put Green Party's demands on fridge 'where everyone can see them'

IT'S almost five months since the 2020 general election and government talks are finally nearing conclusion, as the main parties attempt to coax independents and minority parties into bed like a rouged hoor at a Parisian brothel.

More progress was made on Thursday when Green Party leader and occasional hedgerow sniffer Eamon Ryan presented the leaders of Fianna Fáil and Fine Gael with 17 demands that he had done 'all by myself'.

Micheál Martin made a big deal of looking at the demands, saying, 'Oh these are great, and your handwriting has got so much better too!' Meanwhile Leo Varadkar ruffled Ryan's hair and added, 'I'm going to put this right here on the fridge so that everyone can see them.'

Mr Ryan beamed proudly, saying that his party's position on achieving zero per cent on carbon emissions by 2030 was 'ambitious but doable', to which the Mr Varadkar repeated 'right here on the fridge', while sticking the document to the door with a magnet he'd got as a souvenir of the Camino.

Rustling in his pockets, Mr Martin admitted he was out of change but promised 'something nice' later if Mr Ryan was good, adding, 'Do you need me to drop you home?'

'I have my bicycle,' Mr Ryan said proudly, as he was ushered quickly out the door, both leaders apologising for the rush as they were expecting Mattie McGrath within half an hour and needed to 'doll themselves up'.

'This is so unexpected!' Micheál Martin finally gets job he's actively pursued for last decade

PERENNIAL governmental bridesmaid Micheál Martin finally ascended the throne of Taoiseach yesterday in a traditional ceremony consisting of him being hoisted aloft on the shoulders of the Fianna Fáil parliamentary party in the National Convention Centre, so that 'God could get a better look at him'.

Deposited gracefully on the dais, and wearing his usual mask of a forced smile that would haunt the dreams of any child, he addressed his party and socially distanced members of the press, while clutching a bouquet of lilies and wearing a sash that read 'Best Leader Evs'.

'This is so unexpected,' he gushed, the dust shaking from the diamond-encrusted tiara on his head. 'I just want to thank everyone who made this possible. Fine Gael and the suck…the Greens, my own party, whom I've just sold down the river for the sake of my career. But especially I'd like to thank the people of my constituency, who were willing to overlook the fact I was in government during the worst financial collapse this country has ever known, just so their interests could be represented at a government level.'

His next job will be to appoint his cabinet. 'I've an embarrassment of riches,' he admitted before travelling to the Áras to receive his medal of office and give Michael D. Higgins a sock. 'Dara, Thomas, Barry…someone's going to be disappointed but I'm sure they'll be mature about it.'

Dublin man happy he's solved health crisis by clapping

DARREN FOLEY was beside himself with a sense of achievement last night after solving Ireland's decades-long health crisis by participating in a nationwide minute's clapping in support of frontline health workers.

'I had seen all these posts on social media saying how nurses and doctors were heroes and I just wanted to show my appreciation. I mean, it clashed with a Zoom pub quiz I had arranged but it was a sacrifice I was willing to make.'

Afterwards, Darren described feeling overcome with emotion. 'I mean, it wasn't just me clapping, there were thousands of people doing it. But I felt I really gave it my all, worked the palms and wrists hard. And when I finished, I had this sense of achievement. That's when I knew. Everything was fixed. I'd done it.'

Speaking from his 500,000-euro one-bedroom cottage in Stoneybatter, Darren was elated but critical of government health policy to date.

'While I'm delighted at what I've achieved for Ireland, I think it really highlights the inefficiencies in government. I mean, the Department of Health have spent billions of euro trying to solve the trolley crisis and staffing issues when all they had to do was put their hands together in a clapping motion for a minute to sort it all out.'

When asked if he would be supporting any future pay rises for medical healthcare staff, he said he wouldn't, but that he would be happy to provide workers with a written confirmation of his participation in the clapping in case they could use it to pay their rent or feed their families. Darren is now turning his hands to another serious issue plaguing the country: homelessness.

'Obviously I'm not naïve enough to think something that complex can be solved by clapping. That's why I'm going to dab instead.'

Don Conroy fired after first day on new job

POPULAR cartoonist Don Conroy was left heartbroken yesterday after being fired from his new job after mere hours.

The former *Dempsey's Den* contributor had happily found work as a sketch artist with An Garda Síochána and was looking forward to drawing on his years of experience to help fight crime.

'It's been hard to find work ever since Zag overdosed on ketamine at my house in 1992. So I know how lucky I was to get this job and I was looking forward to making a good impression.'

The day started promisingly enough, gardaí who had grown up with the nineties icon asking him about his days on *The Den* and whether Ian Dempsey had legs or not.

'It was really nice to reminisce,' he admitted.

Then the real work began.

'It was a mugging. The young lady they brought in was understandably upset so they gave her a cup of tea and I sat down with her and asked her to describe her assailant.'

The lady did so: a slight man in his early twenties with blue eyes, cropped hair and a tattoo on his neck. Don had all the details he needed and completed his sketch.

'I showed her the sketch and asked, "Is this the man who stole your phone?" and she said no. When I asked why she said, "Because that's an owl."'

The artist looked again and saw that he had indeed drawn an owl.

'I was mortified. I apologised and asked if we could start again. She agreed and I started over, this time paying even more attention to each detail she gave me.'

He showed her the new drawing and, again, she confirmed he had drawn an owl, although this time he had managed to get the neck tattoo right.

At this stage, the victim requested another artist while Don was taken to see the senior garda in charge.

'He asked me if there was a problem. I asked him did they have many crimes committed by owls. He said there were less than you'd think. Then I admitted that, yes, there was a problem.'

Mr Conroy was released from his contract and returned home. But it's not all bad news.

'I've since had some interest from Dublin City Council who are looking to establish a task force to deal with hordes of marauding seagulls. I can do them. I've already sketched one robbing a *jambon* from a child.'

Gardaí use trail of sourdough starters to trap holiday home owners in West Cork

FEARING the spread of COVID-19 this Easter weekend, gardaí are employing a number of ground-breaking techniques to stop members of the public travelling to their holiday homes, *Mallow News* reports.

In defiance of travel restrictions, hundreds of holidaymakers are expected to make their way to coastal areas to enjoy the warm weather and generally be all-round douches.

Gardaí were quick to act. A trail of sourdough starters, leading from all major motorways to West Cork garda stations, has already netted results, with scores of would-be merrymakers taking the bait, ending up in custody, being fined and sent back to the gilet-wearing community from whence they sprang.

Fresh starters are being provided by local bakers, in partnership with the recently formed Really Irate Residents Association, or RIRA.

Additionally, the force are also using human radar to help echo-locate non-locals in the area. We talked to Garda Tony Law in Clonakilty to learn more.

'Basically, what I do is I roll down the window of the car and shout the opening line of 'Ireland's Call'. Their kind can't resist it. As soon as I hear "shoulder to shoulder", I gun the car and head in that direction. I caught a load of Dermots on their way to Inchydoney yesterday and fined them on the spot.'

Colleagues in Wexford have had similar success, he says, replacing 'Ireland's Call' with 'Sweet Caroline'.

Speaking from his second home in the Phoenix Park, Taoiseach Leo Varadkar applauded the garda initiatives but advised caution.

'These measures should be for working-class people on their way to wheely-houses and should not hinder proper people, like judges or Fine Gael party members, from visiting and maintaining their holiday homes,' he said.

Aware that the restrictions may still be in place by the May bank holiday weekend, gardaí have recommended that, in future, all roadblocks be manned by the Revenue Commissioners instead.

Coronavirus finds cure for dreadful plague – gives loyalists their marching orders

IT WAS a case of 'Yes, surrender!' in Belfast yesterday as the grand mandarin of the Orange Order announced that the traditional Twelfth of July celebrations had been cancelled due to restrictions on public gatherings put in place to stop the spread of another terrible dose, COVID-19.

'It is with great regret that we must cancel the 2020 Boyne anniversary parades. We would ask our members to self-distance and practise bigotry in their own homes instead. Maybe by trolling James McClean on Twitter or ringing *The Nolan Show*. Every little helps,' said Grand Wizard Kyle Hatred.

In addition to the parades being cancelled, the order has also advised both unionist and loyalist communities to refrain from participating in their Eleventh Night bonfires. 'I appreciate that our tradition and culture of burning people in effigy and releasing enough carbon emissions to make Greta Thunberg cry are very much our way of life, but we would urge people to stay in and not give in to temptation,' cautioned local DUP councillor Jimmy Gout.

It is hoped that technology may be used to hold virtual bonfires but emergency services are concerned people will simply set their laptops on fire.

The economic impact of the cancellations is significant, with workers in Northern Ireland's booming pallet-thieving industry now left unemployed. 'Financial aid from the Tories is vital,' said Councillor Gout, 'but every time Arlene tries contacting Westminster all she gets is a message saying, "New phone, who dis?"'

Meanwhile, the Catholic community has responded positively to the news, praising the Orange Order's newfound maturity and awarding coronavirus the freedom of the city of Derry.

Three ghosts of Christmas declare Eoghan Murphy 'a lost cause'

THE three supernatural manifestations of Christmas today revealed that they were officially declaring housing minister Eoghan Murphy a lost cause after yet another unsuccessful intervention.

This is the second year in a row where the spirits have failed to convince the fresh-faced landlord fluffer of the need to rehabilitate his life or face a future of certain misery and loneliness.

'It's been heartbreaking really,' said the Ghost of Christmas Past. 'I've shown him visions of his formative years where he built Lego houses and charged his sister's dolls rent, thinking it would make him reconsider. He just marvelled at his naivety, saying, "I should have charged them more based on the market rate."'

The Ghost of Christmas Present was equally disheartened. 'I took him through the streets of Dublin and showed him the masses gathering in doorways for warmth, the children celebrating Christmas in an overcrowded hotel room. He actually giggled and asked if he could get a DVD of the vision.'

Typically, the most successful of the triad, the Ghost of Christmas Future, faced the same frustrations as his brothers. 'I brought him 20 years into the future. Showed him his older self, sitting on a throne of bones in the abandoned Dublin City Council whitewater rafting facility, surrounded by a mob of mutants on water-skis eager to go on a Great Hunt into the flooded city centre. When I looked over, expecting him to be in tears, he was taking pictures with his iPhone and posting them to his Instagram account with the hashtag #lifegoals.'

The ethereal beings say they are now focusing on less challenging projects such as convincing Phil Hogan to resign or keeping Eamon Ryan awake.

Irish government agrees Mrs Brown's Boys sufficient reparations for occupation

TAOISEACH Micheál Martin signed an agreement with human bath bomb Boris Johnson yesterday that formally outlines UK reparations for their 800-year occupation of Ireland.

The 100-page document outlines that the UK government would finally admit to the hurt and damage caused by years of subjugation of the Irish people and their culture and would, in return, formally take ownership and responsibility for *Mrs Brown's Boys*.

The deeply unfunny and offensive prime minister said this was an opportunity for both countries to strengthen ties and put past enmities behind them. 'There is more that unites us than separates us,' he said. 'For ex-ample, I love potatoes and bathing only once a month.'

As of today, all cast members and crew of the popular BBC show will have their nationality changed to British and have all records expunged from the National Archive of Ireland in Dublin.

It is believed that earlier drafts of the agreement had attempted to force the British to repatriate Nathan Carter as well as take responsibility for other un-wanted Irish talent.

'We tried to play hardball and get them to take Ryan Tubridy too,' admitted Minister Simon Coveney, 'but the prime minister thought that the British public would be more open to another decade of austerity instead.'

Phil Hogan in lockdown trip to Dublin to wipe his arse on the Book of Kells

EU TRADE Commissioner and Ireland's very own littlest hobo Phil Hogan was once again in the spotlight yesterday as more details of his lockdown transgressions were made public.

In a further apology issued from his office, Mr Hogan admitted making a trip to Dublin to wipe his arse on the historic Book of Kells at Trinity College.

'I was unaware that this is not common practice, as it is something we do all the time in Kilkenny,' he stated. 'To be honest, I had meant to do it with the Constitution but unfortunately the National Library was closed.'

The former Fine Gael TD also admitted to several additional stops before his return to the K Club in Kildare.

'On my way back, I made a brief stopover in the Áras to feed dark chocolate to the presidents' dogs, opened five hotels and convinced RTÉ to commission a new series starring Jason Byrne.'

Mr Hogan remained adamant that he did not breach public health advice, claiming that the HSE website clearly does not advise against Irish citizens helping Jason Byrne's career.

'I'm being made a scapegoat,' he muttered darkly, adding, 'there were people far more important than me at that dinner. Brian Hayes, Jerry Buttimer, Cthulhu to name but a few. You don't see them being crucified. If you'll excuse me, I have to take this call.'

Phil Hogan's fate now rests squarely in the hands of European Commission President Ursula von der Leyen, who says she will at least read his account of the affair before demanding his resignation.

Mattie McGrath asks army to intervene after hour goes missing

INDEPENDENT Tipperary TD and sour-faced pro-life onion bucket Mattie McGrath yesterday appealed to the Taoiseach to mobilise the army to investigate the disappearance of an hour over the weekend.

'This happens every year in March and I'm sick shit of it,' he raged in the Dáil. 'The army need to get off their arses and come down to Tipperary and find it. I can't just wait until October for it to come back like a stray cat.'

Mr McGrath explained that he had missed three funerals, two weddings, a witch-burning and a bar mitzvah due to the 'time shenanigans' and would be seeking state compensation for the potential vote loss come the next general election.

He found support in the form of fellow independent Michael Healy-Rae, who said his poor brother took to the fields and hasn't been seen in days. 'We could do with the Army Rangers coming down with a few dogs to track him,' he admitted.

Taoiseach Micheál Martin assured both members that there was a perfectly reasonable scientific explanation for all of this, at which stage they stormed out of the Dáil, with McGrath warning him that if he wanted to count on their support during the next vote of no-confidence he'd want to 'come down off his high horse'.

Hours later troops arrived in Thurles and were seen beating the hedges and walking the fields around the area.

'Fair play to Mattie,' said one local. 'He showed them boys we're no fools,' adding that he hoped to use the extra time to catch up on his Angelus.

PSNI safely detonate Sammy Wilson

SAMMY WILSON, DUP MP and love-child of a strawberry and an aneurysm, was safely detonated by the PSNI yesterday after concerns he might finally explode.

Members of the PSNI bomb-disposal unit were alerted by concerned members of the public and rushed to Stormont, where Mr Wilson was addressing his fellow assembly members.

'We think the trigger was a discussion on climate change,' said bomb-disposal specialist James Gordon. 'When we arrived, he was screaming that Greta Thunberg was "the devil in pigtails" and that the only child we should listen to was the "baby Jesus".'

Using the standard issue DUP rage colour chart, he discovered that Mr Wilson was a shade called 'abortion rights red' and made the call to have him removed from the building.

'I knew time was of the essence. I've only seen one other case like this, in *Chernobyl*, the TV show. We lured him out by convincing him that there was a hedge in the gardens that looked like King Billy.'

They were just in time.

'A group of Irish Language Act advocates were gathered on the steps. It was enough to send him over the edge.'

The detonation was heard all over Belfast. Miraculously, no one was harmed, not even Mr Wilson.

'We think his skin is some kind of asbestos-gammon hybrid,' said a doctor from the Royal Victoria Hospital. 'It's really quite remarkable.'

Responding to Sinn Féin's accusations that Mr Wilson's behaviour threatened the peace process, the DUP promised to make sure he would be put beyond use at the earliest opportunity.

Irish alt right publish convenient list of things only proud bog-born patriots can do

IRELAND'S National Party, a political group dedicated to protecting the racial purity of a people who look like albino potatoes, today published what they called a 'definitive' list of activities that can only be pursued by people born and inbred in Ireland. Party leader Justin Barrett said the list is a useful guide to maintaining the 'integrity' of Ireland's culture. The list includes:

1 **Irish dancing:** Invented by fair maidens queuing for toilets at a crossroads. Any attempt to modernise it with foreign music or steps is a direct attack on Ireland's chastity.

2 **Hurling:** This attack sport invented by ISPCA founder Cúchulainn is for Irish people only. Foreign blood will only dilute the pure MiWadi of this game.

3 **Fruit-picking/manual labour:** Irish jobs for Irish people! We should have the divine right to turn down jobs we wouldn't touch with a barge pole.

4 **Social welfare:** Claiming social welfare can be traced all the way back to Brian Boru and the Battle of Clontarf. Today, it's the massed ranks in Premier League jerseys shouting for foreigners to get out who need our support. Patriotism is a full-time job and should be subsidised by the state.

5 **Making love:** Only Irish men should make love to Irish women and vice-versa. God be with the days when women didn't have a choice.

6 **Boiled and fried food:** Rice has no place in Ireland, neither does spice. If it's not brown or white, then it's awful shite. No to foreign muck. An excited palate has no place in our society.

7 **Trad music:** Ireland's answer to jazz was invented to drive the British away from our shores. It's already polluted by the bouzouki, a creeping replacement that must be stopped.

The list has been published on the party's website, whiteireland.ie, and is also available from bus station toilets throughout the country.

'We're not in the business of attending the sick' – Catholic Church warns the ill to avoid mass

A SPOKESMAN for the Catholic Diocese of Cloyne today encouraged members of the faithful to avoid going to mass due to the ongoing coronavirus crisis.

Preying especially on the vulnerable and the elderly, the Catholic Church is one of the first institutions to voice its concerns about the disease.

Speaking at a press conference, the spokesman described ill people as 'gross' and 'sticky' and said that if God meant for priests to grant succour to the sick and the dying, he would surely have written it down somewhere, in 'like the Bible or something'. 'In an ideal world we would like to wave a magic wand and make this illness disappear but, in fairness, we might as well try to move it to another parish,' he added. He then pleaded with locals not to use holy water as a preventative measure as it has no antibacterial properties and is 'only tap water that's had a bit of a pray over it'.

In guidance issued to parishes, vulnerable churchgoers have been informed that they can still attend mass via Skype and can also receive communion via DeliverYou.

Today's statement comes after last week's cancellation of the sign of peace handshake, which has now been replaced by an arched eyebrow of mutual respect and a gentle puff on the back of your neighbour's neck.

Leaving Cert cancelled and replaced with Winning Streak

THOUSANDS of students were put out of their misery yesterday when the Minister for Education finally cancelled this year's Leaving Cert examinations.

Minister Joe McHugh announced that, instead, students would be entitled to spin a Wheel O'Points™ on an extra-special episode of RTÉ's *Winning Streak*.

Speaking at Leinster House, Minister McHugh, who looks like he attended school in a burrow, said that students would be allocated a time slot on the show and be able to instruct host Marty Whelan – virtually – to spin the wheel on their behalf. Whatever slot the ball finally landed in would be the total number of CAO points the student would be entitled to.

Many students were overjoyed at the news, especially given the uncertainty of the past two months.

'This is a completely arbitrary approach to deciding our future,' said one delighted teen, 'so it's just as good as the Leaving.'

Others were not so happy. Representatives from a parents' group accosted the minster after the press conference complaining that this approach was unfair, as they had spent thousands on private grinds to ensure their offspring would get the points they needed. Mr McHugh was quick to reassure them that students from better performing schools would be able to keep spinning until they got the points they needed, maintaining the status quo and ensuring that no undesirables would be sitting next to their little darlings as they pretend to study English Literature at Trinity.

'Closure of Bewley's another nail in cultural coffin,' says columnist who hasn't been inside it in a decade

FORMER culchie tea-and-bun house Bewley's announced yesterday that it was to close permanently due to high rents and the fact that consumers now have options. Talking to *Mallow News,* opinion columnist and author of *City of Hotels: No Culture No Cry* Nuala Frown said that this was another example of Dublin's cultural heart being ripped from its rotting body.

'Bewley's is a landmark, a reminder of simpler times when simple working-class people would gather to marvel at things they could only dream of, like cake and indoor plumbing. The beauty of the building was a tonic against the high-street monuments to Konsumor, the Celtic god of capitalism, whose tongue lapped ever greedily at Bewley's shores.'

The closure has been attributed to the 1.5 million euro annual rent charged by Ronan Real Estate Group, a company run by Johnny Ronan, a property developer, and testament to the claim money is an aphrodisiac.

'Men like him are the Antichrist,' Ms Frown continued.

'We are now engaged in a cultural jihad. Clubs and bars are being torn down and replaced by hotels and apartments, without a thought for where me and my friends can go for a drink. At this rate, I might have to go to the northside. It's inhumane.'

When asked what she would miss most about Bewley's, the two-time winner of the Perfunctorily Woke Writer of the Year Award became contemplative. 'I haven't been there in years, but I will miss the concept of it, which is more tangible in a way, really.'

CITY OF

HOTELS:

NO CULTURE

NO CRY

Nuala Frown

Man in direct provision can't wait for lockdown to end so he can return to normality of lockdown

QUARANTINE has been hard for many in Irish society, and Hassan El Fateh is no exception. Having fled his native Syria in 2019, he claimed asylum in Ireland and ended up in the warm corporate embrace of our direct provision system.

Assigned to a hotel in Tralee, Hassan admits his first impression wasn't that positive. 'I asked, "When was your war?" I was about to give the manager some money as a donation when he pointed out that the city has always looked like this. But the locals could not have been more welcoming, standing outside the hotel with lovely signs. My written English is not so good, but I assume the slogans were all about inclusivity and how the Irish recognise that they have been immigrants themselves and can empathise with my situation.'

Hassan quickly got into the daily rhythm of having no agency and staring at four walls for days on end. 'It remind-ed me of my time in prison,' he recalls fondly, 'only the food there was edible.'

Not wanting to appear ungrateful, he points out that at least there is no physical torture. 'The soles of my feet were beaten and burned by the army, which was unbelievably painful. All I have to deal with here is the psychological damage caused by the unceasing boredom and uncertainty of this Kafkaesque system that you Irish have created, this perversion of your *céad míle fáilte*. I apologise again for my rough English,' he adds.

Lockdown has been difficult for Hassan. 'I've found it hard to not look for jobs I'm not entitled to,' he admits. 'Plus, a lot of the locals think we in DP are infected with the virus, despite the fact we've all been self-isolating for years. So, it will be nice when the restrictions are lifted and we can go back to being ignored.'

Off-licences seek government subsidy after Junior Cert cancelled

AFTER what has easily been the longest April on record [citation needed], the government has finally made the decision to cancel the Junior Certificate, undoing all the hard work of Irish parents who spent the last year convincing their children that this arbitrary workfest was 'an integral part of their educational career'.

However, this decision was not met with universal cheer, as members of the Irish Federation of Off-Licences castigated the Department of Education's decision, saying that the focus on children was 'admirable' but 'misguided'.

'The real victims here are the owners and operators of Ireland's off-licences,' said Francis Crowley, chairperson of the federation. 'We depend heavily on young teenage drinkers to keep our industry afloat. Now, more than ever, we need financial aid to help get us through this troubling time.

'Junior Cert results night is typically an opportunity for our members to offload stock that normally doesn't sell, to underage drinkers who don't know any better,' he added. 'Now, the children will be staying indoors, spending time with their families rather than vomiting and making terrible personal choices.

'It's a constitutional rite of passage for young teenagers to get absolutely skullponged on cheap alcohol,' he continued. 'Without this, they may never make the important leap to regular heavy drinking like the generations before them. This could be the beginning of the end for our industry,' wailed Mr Crowley, clutching a tricolour.

Independent politicians have supported the federation's request, with local TD

and publican Mattie Singleton commenting, 'Look, we all know the legal age for drinking is 18, but a recent study published by the Irish Vintners Association shows that age is really 14 when you take into account Irish genetics. So basically, if you deny a child access to alcohol, you're in breach of the law.'

The Department of Health has said it will consider the request as soon as lobbyists have made clear how much they can make it worth their while.

...ment commits to making homeless contactless payment compliant by 2020

THE Irish government has outlined a new initiative to help tackle Ireland's chronic homelessness problem by promising to provide access to contactless payment by late 2020.

The initiative, in partnership with AIB and Bank of Ireland, would see homeless people voluntarily fitted with receivers that would allow members of the public to transfer up to 30 euro per transaction.

'This has all the convenience of donating money only without the danger of actual physical contact,' said housing minister Eoghan Murphy, smiling like a shark at a sushi bar.

'Of course this service is not free,' added Minister for Finance Paschal Donohoe, 'they must also consent to be fitted with wi-fi transmitters, as we have reached an agreement with the nation's leading broadband providers to use the homeless as mobile hotspots so that tourists and young professionals can log in and access high-speed internet. They can then choose to donate afterwards.

'We see this as only the beginning in an attempt to commodify our most vulnerable,' he continued. 'Imagine thousands of homeless people wearing Google-branded clothing. We've also had some very interesting conversations with the makers of Pokémon GO.'

When asked by members of the media if the initiative was potentially dehumanising, Minister Murphy said that, as far as he was concerned, this would provide homeless people with a chance to earn money without the government directly providing them with accommodation as 'houses are for real people'.

Ireland's criminal gangs suspend rivalry to ensure steady supply of drugs

KEY players in the Hutch–Kinahan feud met secretly yesterday to agree a temporary ceasefire in order to ensure that illegal-drug users across the country could count on a steady supply during the lockdown.

Observing social distancing, and with the additional protection of masks behind their balaclavas, the gangs agreed to suspend the feud that had consumed them for the past five years, bumping elbows to seal the truce.

'We need to come together, you know, without blowing each other apart,' sniffed a representative from the Hutch family.

A member of the Kinahans agreed. 'We're putting the violence behind us for a month or two for the good of the community. After all, we're Irish first, murderous bastards second.'

Members of the public, legal industry and media welcomed the ceasefire because, as one anonymous local newspaper editor put it, 'Daddy needs fuel for his brain train, baby, and it's choo-choo time!'

A garda representative told *Mallow News* that the move wasn't entirely unwelcome.

'It's hard enough stopping Sorchas and Dermots from cycling on footpaths without having to mop up a crime scene or deal with some young lad trying to snort a DVD copy of *Scarface* in a desperate attempt to get high.'

The gangs reassured members of the public that as soon as the lockdown was over, they would return to their mindless murdering.

Man about to serenade apartment block with 'Galway Girl' taken out by sniper

NOT all heroes wear capes. Some wear camouflage jackets and night-vision goggles, waiting patiently on rooftops around Ireland's cities, ready to leap into action at a moment's notice.

Corporal Danny Higgins, Army Rangers sniper, was deployed to Cork city two days ago as part of a government initiative to protect citizens from another insidious plague that has spread throughout the country since lockdown: impromptu public performances of popular music.

The phenomenon started in Italy and Spain and soon spread to Ireland, where innocent members of the public trapped in their homes were subjected to aural waterboarding by tone-deaf minstrels anxious to raise spirits and their social-media profiles.

Today's perpetrator was Bernard Staunton, an IT consultant and self-described 'old soul'.

In an act of terrible cruelty, Bernard had been told by some friends that he had a real talent for the acoustic guitar and should consider 'turning professional'. According to posts on his Facebook page, he was excited to showcase his talents and 'bring joy' to the hundreds of people in his city-centre apartment block with a cover of Ed Sheeran's musical hate crime 'Galway Girl'.

He made it as far as the opening verse before a crack shot from the concealed sniper severed the neck of his guitar and another significantly wounded his picking hand.

'The horrors I've seen in Liberia or Su-

dan pale in comparison to the damage a misplaced Gavin James or Dermot Kennedy cover can do to a residential area,' Corporal Higgins told *Mallow News* afterwards.

As Mr Staunton was removed to hospital, neighbours approached the Army Ranger to shake his hand and thank him for his service.

'I'm just glad to do my duty,' he said, as a helicopter arrived to transfer him to Dublin, where a clearly intoxicated Bono had just been seen dancing on the roof of the Clarence Hotel.

Eamon Ryan to collaborate with Versatile on musical apology for use of the N-word

GREEN Party leader and secondary-school teacher who desperately wants you to like him Eamon Ryan today announced his intention to collaborate with Irish rappers Versatile on a musical apology for his recent use of the N-word in Dáil Éireann.

Mr Ryan came under fire last Thursday when he read out a newspaper article on the scourge of racism that contained the notorious racial slur. Anti-racism groups across the country described his actions as thoughtless and insensitive, with members of his own party calling for an apology. He issued a brief statement soon after, recognising that he was 'completely wrong' to use the word.

In a longer, more considered statement he announced his intention to offer a more appropriate expression of his regret.

'I realise that music can say much more than a written apology ever could,' he said at a press conference from his south Dublin home, 'so I picked up the old acoustic guitar and just started speaking my truth. The words just flowed out of me like a reclaimed water pipe.'

His advisor Barry (a psychic parrot) counselled him to work with young rappers Versatile so that he could connect with younger voters.

The Irish rap duo, who sound like the cast of *Love/Hate*, jumped at the opportunity to collaborate with the Green Party leader saying, 'One of us will, loike, be Minister for Health in the near future, roight? So it's good to make connections.'

The apology song, entitled 'No Black or White, Just Green', will be released next week, with all proceeds going to a new charity Mr Ryan has established called Allotments for Racially Sensitive Environmentalists, or ARSE.

In the meantime, Mr Ryan will face a leadership challenge from deputy leader Catherine Martin, who is currently adopting the Machiavellian approach of just letting her boss say whatever the fuck pops into his busy little brain.

2020 Rose of Tralee to be held on abandoned oil rig off coast of Yemen

THE summer season of festivals was effectively cancelled this week with the government announcement that gatherings of 5,000 people or more were prohibited until the end of August, as part of the fight against the spread of the coronavirus.

Middle-aged men across Ireland were left heartbroken at the prospect of sitting at home taking yokes and watching Ryan Tubridy instead of going to music festivals and momentarily thinking they were still young. Racing fans were left bereft at the notion of getting further in debt at home instead of at the track.

Equally distraught were the people of Tralee at the notion that their internationally famous personality contest would be cancelled.

'The local economy depends on the Rose festival,' said local TD Conor Shannon. 'It's the second largest source of income, after whinging.'

Luckily, help was at hand in the unexpected form of a Saudi Arabian prince.

'Prince Ali rang me on the mobile, he got my number off Mattie McGrath. It turns out he was a fan of the contest since he was a teenager and wanted to do what he could to help. It's like a fairy tale!'

The prince proposed holding the contest in international waters on an abandoned oil rig he uses occasionally for paintballing and private executions. The event would be streamed online with a portion of the streaming rights reverting to Tralee Town Council.

'There will have to be some changes, of course,' admitted Mr Shannon. 'The girls will have to wear more clothing and if the escorts try any saucy business they'll be thrown in prison. In a lot of ways, we're taking the contest back to its roots.'

Irish fans of the show needn't worry about too much change with Dáithí Ó Sé presenting as usual. 'I haven't seen the location yet, but the prince has promised a virtual tour on Zoom, as soon as his cleaners have removed the

stains from last month's MMA tourna-ment,' he announced on Twitter.

Amnesty International have con-demned the move, citing the kingdom's long history of human rights abuses.

'Sure, they say that every year,' Mr Shannon countered, 'and that hasn't stopped us.'

Sunburned Dub to be used as renewable energy source

FÉLIM MURPHY from Coolock made his annual pilgrimage to the beach yesterday, delighting all and sundry with his display of translucent flesh on the DART, before emerging like a bi-pedal jellyfish onto the beach at Portmarnock and looking forward to the kiss of the sea spray on his skin and the scent of raw sewage in his nostrils.

Sadly, within 15 minutes he had suffered a sunburn so comprehensive that it covered his entire body, with the exception of the parts covered by his shorts and his miraculous medal, which was now embedded so deep within his crispy flesh that only a future king of England could remove it.

Brought by ambulance to Beaumont Hospital, he was hydrated, assessed by doctors and found to be an ideal candidate for a new government initiative.

Entitled Project Lobster, the scheme aims to repurpose sunburned locals and use their radioactive dermis as a source of renewable energy for Fingal County.

Recruited from local beaches, canals and football matches, the project volunteers act as human power rods, inserted into a uranium core in a facility located next to the new national children's hospital.

Professor Tom Nature, who leads the programme, admitted that the volunteers were in a great deal of pain but were well compensated with an hourly wage of €10.50, a whopping 40 cents above the minimum wage. In addition, they can expect to have all funeral costs covered, although they will need to be buried in concrete so that their bodies don't contaminate the soil and ground water.

'I'm in tremendous pain,' Félim told *Mallow News* via a radio link from the power core. 'I signed a release form while I had heatstroke and now I'm property of the state. It's a disgrace. I'm a man, for fuck sake. Not a single mother.'

Meanwhile, experts predict that if we have a good summer that lasts more than two weeks, Ireland may become energy self-sufficient by 2025.

No vaccine for second wave of terrible plague

DESPITE warnings from experts, the Irish public was left reeling today as it was hit by a second wave of a Fine Gael/Fianna Fáil government.

Having previously been in power together, under the guise of a confidence and supply agreement, it was hoped that the results of the recent general election would stop the spread of the infection but, unfortunately, that was not to be the case.

Public-health experts agreed they had been too slow to act, admitting that, with hindsight, cocooning the elderly before the election would have helped prevent this tragic situation from occurring again.

Those immune to the virus, such as landlords, lobbyists and members of the professional classes, will still be able to go about their business as normal, while those with pre-existing conditions, such as poverty or youth, are advised to stay indoors, and just weather this out.

Key to the success of this wave is political sacrificial lamb the Green Party. Their leader Eamon Ryan was in jubilant form as he addressed members of the media at Government Buildings.

'This is an opportunity for environmental policies to finally take centre stage,' he claimed, gently covering himself in mint sauce.

'I look forward to working with Micheál and Leo when they turn their phones back on.' He then left to select the most appropriate electric bus under which to throw his party come the inevitable collapse of this government.

Until then, the nation is in shock at a return to economic lockdown.

'I thought we did everything right,' said one stunned local. 'I voted left, stayed indoors and just hoped they'd go away. But it just goes to show, until we develop a vaccine, no one's safe.'

Luke 'Ming' Flanagan opens OnlyFans account

INDEPENDENT MEP, former Roscommon TD and the friend in college who always had weed but no rollies Luke 'Ming' Flanagan has set up an OnlyFans account after footage of him appearing bottomless at a European Parliament agriculture committee Zoom meeting went viral yesterday.

Mr Flanagan almost displayed his own independent member when, having been given the floor by the committee chair, it was revealed that he was dressed formally from the bottom up and sex-casual from the bottom down.

Seemingly unaware of his state of *dishabille*, he continued to speak while those on the call stifled laughter and arousal. 'Things are a lot harder here in Ireland,' he said, 'we could do with a stimulus package. Why is everybody crying?'

Within minutes of the footage being leaked, it had reached over a hundred thousand views on YouTube and now has its own dedicated channel on PornHub.

Determined to take ownership of his sexuality and make some money at the same time, the politician will post explicit NSFEPC (Not Suitable For European Parliament Committees) content to his OnlyFans account for subscribers hungry to see more of his milky thighs and tight running shorts.

'I may as well make a few euro out of this while I can,' he told *Mallow News*. 'Mick Wallace has made a fortune on YouTube with his ASMR channel. He plucks his back hair while whispering Seamus Heaney poetry.'

Ming's subscribers already include former European Commission president Jean-Claude Juncker and president of the European Central Bank Christine Lagarde, who told reporters she is thirsty for that 'sweet bog booty'.

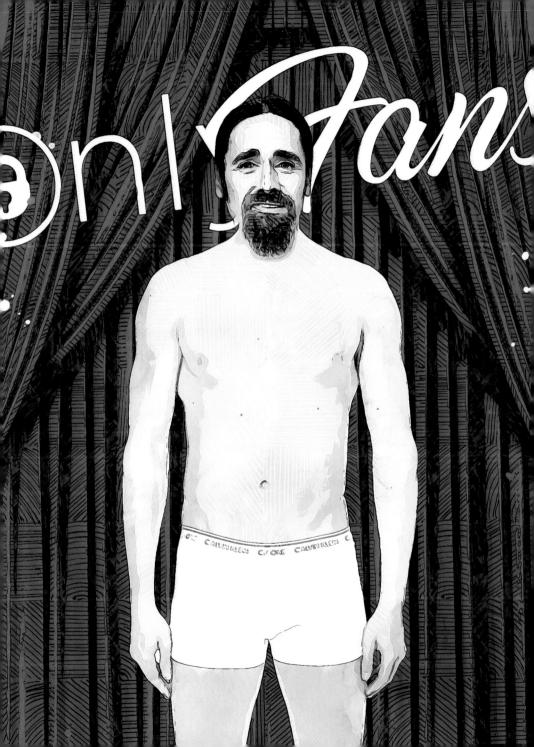

Literary

CORNER

Exclusive extract from latest JCWACG book Part 2

LOCAL author Bernice Browne shot to national fame last year with her debut novel, *Jesus Christ What A Complete Gobnait*, the story of an ordinary girl from Cork called Gobnait, whose warmth, naivety and relatability won a legion of easily impressed fans. The much-anticipated sequel *Wherefore Art Thou, Gobnait?* will be available from 1 April and *Mallow News* is delighted to present this exclusive extract.

I'm wrecked after another long day at work. On my way home, I grab a meal deal for one from Marks & Spencer and a bottle of prosecco, because apparently I should like it even though it tastes like fizzy piss and has the alcohol content of a Guinness fart on a cold night.

Opening the gate to the apartment complex, I stop to hand a euro to Gary the homeless, who is busy having a conversation with the ghost of Michael Collins. Gary is anti-Treaty so it's very sweary. The girls give out to me for giving him money because he only spends it on drink. I mean, fair enough, but he's hardly going to put it towards a deposit or buy shagging prize bonds, like?

'The only pity about this prick,' Gary says, pointing to the empty space next to him, 'is that Dev could have him shot just once.'

'Are you going to a hostel tonight, Gary?' I ask.

'Not likely,' he says. 'I'm fine, but Collins is barred for shitting in the sink.'

'Mind yourself anyway,' I say, closing the gate.

My apartment is a two-bed that I share with a few close friends: Billy, Sharon,

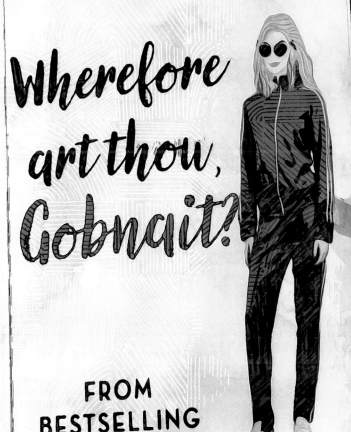

Connie, Jerry, Karen, Kevin, Gay Kevin and Fiona. Ginger Steve went loola last Christmas and now lives in the air-conditioning duct. We have bunk beds in both rooms and a communal living area that consists of a kitchen, two futons and an Ikea couch that Sharon robbed from her ex-boyfriend. We're blessed to have a separate toilet and shower. I know people from home who can basically cook while having a pee.

'You just missed Prendie,' says Kevin, barely looking up from his phone.

Thank Christ. I try to see the best in everyone – it's my thing to be naively optimistic, after all – but Collie Prendeville is one of the worst human beings I've ever met. He's a five-foot five weapon from Togher who cleans his ears with his car keys. He looks like Gollum made out of marla. Normally, I'm not one for judging a book by its cover but Prendie was a first-edition langer. When I viewed the apartment, he spent the whole time looking at my chest, despite the fact that I was wearing a GAA jersey that made me look like a teenage boy with an eating disorder. He offered Karen a 10 per cent discount off her deposit if, and I quote, 'I could give you a deposit of my own, wink wink.'

'What did he want?' I ask, putting my lasagne into the microwave.

'He said he wanted to check the ESB meter but, to be honest, I think he just wanted to perv on Karen.'

That sounded right. Karen was stunning. She was a fragrance girl in BT's, always immaculately turned out, silky hair like a golden cocker spaniel.

'Funny, he always times his visits just when she's getting out of the shower. You'd swear he had cameras in there.'

'That's because he does,' I say, pouring a glass of prosecco. 'Remember, it was a term of our lease?'

My phone buzzes. A notification from Fumble. I open it. 'For feck sake.' Another dick pic. Why do lads think that's sexy? If you're buying meat, you don't go straight to the offal. I delete it and the app. It's too soon anyway. Even though Jerry and I split up after he cheated on me with an Emirates flight attendant, I still have feelings for him and diving back into the dating game isn't smart if my heart isn't in it. After all, I'm not supposed to be into casual flings, as that would probably alienate readers who don't like stirring up complicated feelings they have around women being as sexually free as men.

Will Gobnait find true love again? Will Michael Collins' ghost reveal the Third Secret of Fatima? Will readers still buy this? All these answers and more, in all good bookstores soon.

Horoscopes

WITH TINA PENDRAGON

SHE has many names: sorceress, witch, chartered accountant. Join Tina Pendragon on a journey through the mystery of the stars and beyond. Remember, this is an exact science as proved recently by scientists at MIT (Mallow Institute of Technology).

Aries

Time to stop blaming Cotton Eye Joe for your troubles. The reality is you are a commitment-phobe. Saturn is interfering with your mobile-phone coverage.

Gemini

Time to turn that frown upside down as you decide to get some minor cosmetic surgery. Enjoy some retail therapy by getting a massage in a Centra.

Taurus

As a classic introvert, you Taureans are about to have one hell of a fucking year. The movies of Matt Damon hold a clue for your future.

Cancer

You become increasingly suspicious that everyone else is having a better life than you are. You are correct. Avoid jumping to conclusions about your astrologer wife and her reflexologist.

Leo

You spend too much time worrying about what people think of you when, in reality, they have trouble even remembering your name. Be confident.

Virgo

All work and no play makes Virgoans a dull crowd. It's time to leave the rat race. Badger baiting is much more fun.

Libra

You will accidentally end a work call by telling your manager that you love her and then make it worse by apologising when it becomes clear she never heard you in the first place.

Scorpio

What does not kill you will seriously debilitate you. Love blossoms after a shared glance at the mart.

Sagittarius

Despite having a lactose intolerance, you will insist on eating an ice-cream, thinking that it won't be that bad this time. It will. You swear that you will never do it again. You will.

Capricorn

Prepare for the greatest sex of your life. Maybe next month – it will involve another person.

Aquarius

A problem shared is a problem halved so keep that shit to yourself. Nobody wants half your problems.

Pisces

Time to put those money worries behind you. Call 1580 123 123 (€10 per minute plus network extras) for a personal consultation.

Sport NEWS

Football 'just not the same' without racist chants, bemoans local fan

HOMES across the country resounded once more with the sound of men shouting at millionaire sports players as football finally returned to television screens after an absence of nine weeks.

Taking place behind closed doors, the Bundesliga kicked off proceedings with teams playing to eerily empty stadiums, just like an Athlone Town match.

Normally, Irish football fans wouldn't touch German league football with a shitty stick but, today, they were sucking heartily at its Teutonic teat like an addict trying to get a contact high from a car's exhaust fumes.

One local man didn't share the enthusiasm expressed by his compatriots, however. Harry Mahony (24) had done his best to get into the spirit of things. Surrounded by cans of Bavaria, some Wagner CDs and a couple of tomes that wouldn't look out of place on Michael Gove's bookshelf, he thought he was all set.

But, ten minutes in, he couldn't help but feel there was something missing.

'It just wasn't the same without the terrace bants,' he said, close to tears. 'Half the fun of football is terrorising the black lads but, without the crowds, they were able to play away, unmolested. It's just not right.'

Harry tried shouting his own racist chants at home but realised this was

a side of him his girlfriend hadn't seen, so he shut the fuck up before she threw him out of the house again.

Luckily for Harry, as restrictions ease, he might once again get to enjoy the game he loves. Italy has announced plans for Serie A to restart before the end of June.

'That's like the Premier League for racism and homophobia,' he said, brightening up.

'You can always count on the players to have a go, even if there aren't any crowds.'

GAA Congress 2020 review

THE air was thick with anticipation and the smell of carvery meats as representatives from all over Ireland gathered in Croke Park to participate in the annual GAA Congress, an event that is as transparent and democratic as its delegates are diverse. This year, the congress debated on a total of 64 motions. The following list highlights some of the major changes fans can expect going into this year's sporting calendar.

• Motion 27a was passed, which means Dublin fans are now entitled to claim travel expenses.

• After much debate, the decision to make Lynx Africa the official fragrance of the GAA was unanimously passed.

• In an attempt to mitigate on-pitch confrontations, referees are now required to provide their home addresses to fans.

• A motion to reverse the curse placed on Mayo footballers was defeated, after Marty Morrissey said it would require him to perform multiple forbidden jigs at a crossroads, and his hips were no longer up to the task due to a lifetime of 'fantastic lovemaking'.

• The still-alive portrait of Brian Cody was admitted to the Hall of Fame, to be displayed next to Mickey Harte's final horcrux.

• Under the new Mick Jagger rule, umpires will acknowledge a disallowed point by giving a sassy wagging finger.

• Motion 43, which proposed introducing extra-time in All-Ireland finals to avoid replays, was passed … just kidding, it was defeated and the delegate who proposed it is now living under an assumed name in Panama.

• In order to save time and money, the Dublin football team will now automatically qualify for every All-Ireland final.

• Hawk-Eye's remit is to be extended to include making judgements on players' tattoos.

• The men's urinals in Croke Park have been designated an official wildlife sanctuary.

• The 'sin bin' will be replaced with a confession box.

Britain's Conor McGregor announces retirement from MMA

FIGHTER, businessman and friend to the elderly, Conor McGregor has announced his retirement from Mixed Martial Arts, a sport that's essentially one step up from cock fighting.

McGregor's commitment to the sport has come under fire recently due to his recent match-up against boxer Floyd Mayweather. And, at a press conference from his adopted home of Crumlin in Dublin, Mr McGregor admitted a growing disillusion with the sport had influenced his decision.

'Oi've 'ad it wiv this game, so I 'av,' he said in his native Cockney accent. 'It's no longah the violent, pointless sport oi fell in love wiv.'

The London-born fighter also admitted that it was difficult balancing a career as a fighter with his many business ventures and court appearances.

'It ain't half hard to be a gangstah,' he said, kissing a Union Jack and playfully booting a bulldog up the hole.

It's not the first time McGregor has made an announcement like this, having retired three times already this past month, only to quickly return and use the media attention to launch his latest brand.

When asked if this was just another cynical ploy, McGregor was outraged, flinging pieces of McGregor's Famous Fried Chicken at reporters and storming out to his signature tune 'God Save the Queen'.

John Delaney resigns to spend more time with his money

JOHN DELANEY has resigned his position of Super Handsome Best Executive Vice-President of the Football Association of Ireland with immediate effect.

The FAI confirmed the decision came as a result of mutual agreement and had nothing to do with the string of controversial revelations in the press over the past months that made Delaney and their organisation appear as straight as Quasimodo's spine.

In his statement, written in gold leaf on the cured skin of a white rhino, Mr Delaney said the primary reason for his resignation was personal, that he had neglected that which meant most to him.

'It's far too easy to focus on the material things in life, which is why I want to spend more time with the thousands upon thousands of euro I earned in charge of the FAI. And also my family, I guess.'

The FAI Executive applauded Mr Delaney's work ethic and dedication to football, saying that he is personally responsible for the state of Irish football in the twenty-first century.

Politician and self-described Delaneyite Michael Healy-Rae was inconsolable at the news, telling our reporter that he would be holding a candlelit vigil in Kilgarvan at 8p.m. this Sunday, right after getting a tattoo of Mr Delaney's face on his right buttock.

In terms of next steps for Mr Delaney, it is believed that there is only one place for a man of his considerable experience and personal character, and that members of both Fine Gael and Fianna Fáil have already been in contact.

Mallow to host fourth annual fly-tipping competition

MALLOW will play host to the fourth annual KPMG (Kerry Pig Meat Group) Fly-Tipping All-Ireland final on Saturday, 20 March, with over 20 inter-county fly-tipping All-Stars set to compete on the byways of the town's countryside.

The All-Ireland will determine who is the champion 'discreet disposer of household waste' in the country.

Competitors must attempt to dispose of any type of household waste without being caught by CCTV camera or locals, all of whom will be on high alert as this competition is 'extremely illegal'. Points are given for volume of waste and variety. Mattresses, washing machines and greyhound corpses are all high scorers, although industrial waste is not yet permitted.

The sport has grown in popularity over the past few years, as the privatisation of bin collections and an increase in rates has resulted in the very worst of humanity taking to the countryside and despoiling it rather than spend a few euro and taking their rubbish to the fucking dump.

The current national record is over two tonnes of waste deposited by Waterford man Jason Quinn in a greenway outside Tramore in 2019. Returning to defend his title, Jason said, 'I'm excited to take things to another level this year. I've been filling washing machines with old paint and used nappies for the last month and I've been perfecting my dump 'n' dash moves so that I can win the speed round as well.'

This year's final will also include an excuse round, where competitors are asked to give their bullshit justification for illegal dumping, with extra points awarded for delusion and self-righteousness.

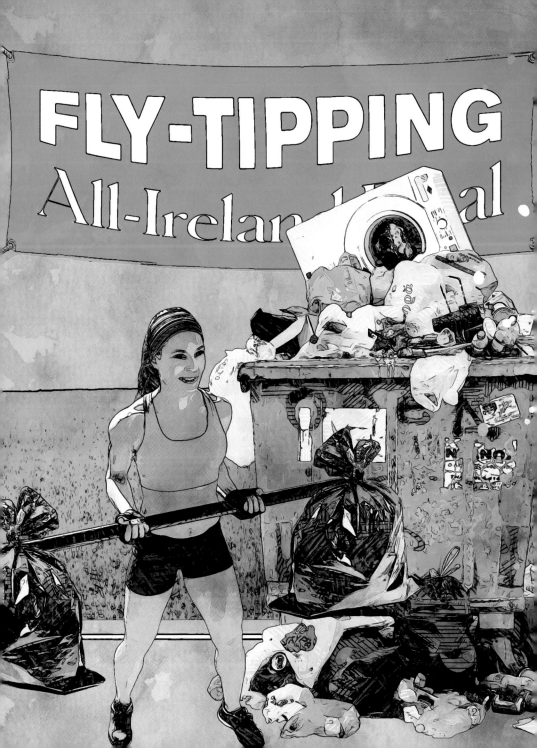

Road Bowling

A QUIET road outside Mallow town. A crowd has gathered. Bets are placed, money changes hands and an occasional discreet sip is taken from a naggin of Powers. There's a buzz of anticipation in the air. Suddenly, all is quiet.

A man approaches the centre of the road, hefting a bowl in his hands. With the body of Bacchus and the keen eyes of Apollo, he surveys the path before him. He takes his time. He begins his approach. Slowly at first, then quicker, until he becomes a blur of limbs like Michael Flatley at a Düsseldorf rave. The bowl is released. He smiles. At what, we will never know because his head then disappears in a mist of blood and brain. The crowd sighs disappointedly and I am inducted into the world of Ultimate Road Bowling.

As Farrow's undertakers quickly remove his headless corpse from the road, I talk to event organiser Darragh Sweeney about the origin of the underground game that is taking Cork's sporting scene by storm.

'I was home from college one week-end and Da (legendary road bowler Liam 'Snack Box' Sweeney) convinced me to go with him to watch him bowl over in Toomevara. On the way out in the car, he started complaining about a pain in his chest, but he just put it down to old age and the 15 *jambons* he'd put away at breakfast that morning. By the time he started his match, he was sweating and panting like a priest in a playground. Halfway through, he collapsed. The crowd suddenly became animated and started making bets on whether or not he would survive. The energy was amazing. As the hearse took him away and I collected my winnings, suddenly, I had an idea that would change my life forever.'

That idea was Ultimate Road Bowling. All the elements of the classic Irish game combined with the danger of sudden, unexpected death.

He takes me through the course later that day. 'So, Timmy, who you saw earlier, his mistake was waiting too long to throw the bowl. He was taken out by Pat here.'

'Hello there!'

I am surprised by a voice coming from a nearby tree. Looking up, I see local gamekeeper Pat Dorney in full camouflage gear, holding a high-powered rifle.

'Jesus, Pat, you put the heart crossways on me.'

'Sorry. How's the form?'

'Not too bad now. What got you into all of this?' I ask.

He tells me that Darragh approached him in the pub and asked him if he was interested in a job shooting the most dangerous game of all. 'I thought he was talking about velociraptors but when he explained to me that he meant people, I said, "Great stuff." I mean, I only think about it every day.'

'That's worrying,' I tell him.

'You're not wrong,' he replies cheerfully, reloading his rifle.

We finish our tour, Darragh asking for my discretion as he doesn't want the course spoiled for future competitors.

Joining him later at his house, I ask him the one question that's been preying on my mind since I crawled out of the quicksand pit and heard a distant explosion that later turned out to be Billy Staunton.

'Isn't this all illegal?' I ask him.

'You'd think so – but, no. All competitors sign a form waiving liability. We pay all the medical and funeral bills. They're all over 66, with pre-existing medical conditions, so the government are more than happy to turn a blind eye.'

'I can see what's in it for you, but what about the bowlers?'

'Adulation, pure and simple. Attendance is through the roof and the lads missed that roar of the crowd. To them it's worth dying for – or at the very least a partial mutilation.'

This is early days for the sport, but Darragh is already looking at expanding his business across all four provinces.

'I see this as having nationwide appeal,' he says, as we chat over tea and biscuits. 'I'm in talks with TG4 for the streaming rights. The GAA have been on to me. A couple of lads in Fine Gael have said it has great potential for solving the current homelessness crisis. Who knows? It could go global.'

Locals wishing to attend the next round of Ultimate Bowling should head out to Farrahy's Lane next Sunday, just follow the old Cork road and take a right at Billy Staunton's severed leg.

Biography review: Scrumface
by Gordon Howth, with Vincent Browne

Former bad boy of 1990s rugby tells all, but should he have, and does anyone care?

FROM The opening paragraph of this autobiography, former Irish rugby star Gordon 'Gee-Bag' Howth lets you know you're in for a whirlwind of action, drama and romance.

After I vomited into a pint glass and then drank it all in one go, I knew I had regained the respect of the dressing room and President Robinson. We were ten points down against the old enemy, *Western Samoa, and I was still high from the night before. As I led the lads in a rousing version of 'Karma Chameleon', the blood began streaming from my nose.*

The boss took me to one side and told me, 'Here's another bump to get you through the second half.'

'Thanks, Mr Haughey,' I said.

The *enfant terrible* of 1990s rugby, Howth was feared both on and off the pitch, winning 75 caps for his country and making 60 appearances for Leinster, where he was captain for their historic cup win over London Asbestos in 1993. In an era when fitness played second fiddle to girth, Howth was an immense presence both on and off the field. His appetite for the game was equalled only by his appetite for other less savoury desires, which he indulged in to great excess and which his former defence solicitor Vincent Browne expertly catalogues in this pacey autobiography from Generic House Press.

From his boarding school days at Clonrock College, playing lumpy wafer with the prefects, to his eventual fall from grace, when he is accused of eating scrum-half Albert Poussain in the 1992 Five Nations decider against France, the narrative never drags and he never flinches from the truth, no matter how revolting.

When I was at Clonrock College, it was tradition for the winning captain to be presented with the Senior Cup by the losing captain's mother. Needless to say, I spent many evenings practising my box kick, if you know what I mean? I had sex with a lot of them is what I mean.

If you're looking for deep introspection, though, this isn't the place to find it.

This is, after all, the player who suffered 18 concussions during a single match, including five as he was trying to leave the changing room after having attended the *Sunday Independent* Christmas party the night before.

Ultimately, he cuts a tragic figure, spending his post-rugby career earning money from letting dwarves kick him in the genitals on cult Ukrainian game show *Gonads* and drunkenly asking Enya to fellate him on an infamous episode of *The Late Late Show*.

His eventual *rapprochement* with the 18 children he fathered – then abandoned – over the years forms a touching coda to the book and leaves the reader with a better taste in their mouth than those he played lumpy wafer with back in his schooldays.

'My online agony'

GAA star opens up after pitch rampage

FERMANAGH defender Senan Brady has admitted being in the public spotlight can be 'stressful' and has cautioned so-called social-media trolls to 'watch what they say' about players unless they want to 'end up six feet under a bog with their feet stuffed in their mouths'.

Brady was retrospectively banned for one match yesterday after an incident in a game against Ulster championship rivals Derry.

A huge debate was sparked online after footage emerged of him decapitating midfielder Mark McCarthy with a samurai sword during the national anthem before proceeding to play the match wearing McCarthy's severed head as a hat.

Sunday Game analysts were particularly scathing, with Joe Brolly calling for Brady's permanent suspension from the championship.

'This behaviour is unacceptable, and something that I would never condone, never mind participate in,' he said on the show, while blood dripped from his own head hat.

Brady apologised after the incident and said in an interview for Lynx Men's *Scents Magazine* that the criticism he had received on Twitter had led to him considering leaving the game permanently.

'People can be very quick to judge you, calling you a murderer and worse just for taking a lad's head off, hai. They need to be very careful as I will find every single one of them and fucking murder them to death,' he said from his court-mandated anger-management class.

'At the end of the day this is just a hobby, not something I do professionally. I still have to go to work every day stunning cows at the local abattoir. It's really made me re-evaluate my life.'

Brady's ban has been appealed by the county board on the grounds that it is 'disproportionate' and that the injured player 'would have died sometime anyway'. The result of the appeal will be known next Wednesday.

Cookery corner
—with Cathy

SPICE BAG

Ingredients
- 1 lb chicken leavings
- 2 tsp mixed spices, whatever you have – don't worry, you won't taste anything
- Ground pepper and salt to taste
- 4 oz plain flour
- ½ tsp baking powder
- 1 red pepper
- 1 green pepper
- 2 large potatoes, chipped
- 6 pints stout
- 2 shots whiskey

AS the nights draw in and our hearts grow colder, I think there's no better winter warmer than my spice bag recipe, which I'll now share with all of you as part of our continuing series of Irish Culinary Treasures.

Spice bags originated in Kildare, where the desperate proprietor of a local Chinese restaurant realised he had run out of chicken balls half an hour before the local GAA club disco was due to finish. In an act of serendipitous madness, he scraped the side of his chip pan, deep fried the contents of his bin and added some mixed peppers and spice to confuse the rural palate into thinking it was eating something authentic. Of course, it proved such a hit that it now graces the menu in most of the country's chippers, whose owners realised very quickly that the margin is fantastic.

Method
I'm not going to lie to you: there's not a lot of nuance here. Heat up your chip pan to 180°C. Feck all the dry ingredients into a Ziploc bag and shake.

Fry until it looks the same shade of greyish-brown as a rural TD having a heart attack.

While the spice bag is cooking, drink all six pints of stout (Murphy's is the number-one choice in our household) and down the two shots of whiskey.

Serving suggestion
As you weave drunkenly throughout your house dropping crispy pieces of spicy disappointment, you'll appreciate that looks aren't everything and that the spice bag is the culinary equivalent of the desperate last-minute shift in a nightclub on Stephen's Night. Put it in a bag or a bowl, it doesn't matter – you've committed to eating it and you'll cope with the consequences in the morning.

Love, Cathy

Lifestyle NEWS

AND ENTERTAINMENT

Ocras! The Musical
Jaunty local production that leaves you hungry for more

BY FÉILIM COURTNEY

WHILE her husband toils the stony, unforgiving ground of their tenant farm in Connemara, Noneen Ní Capall teaches Irish and passive-aggressiveness at the local hedge school, trying to fight off the not-unwelcome advances of StepJoy Mounthenry, the cruel but handsome landlord, who threatens to reveal the school's location to the British army unless she submits to his will.

Meanwhile, the annual potato crop is failing and while starvation grips the country, Noneen finds herself facing yet further temptations, more dark than she could ever imagine. Songs such as 'Blight Eyes' and 'What's the Story (Harvest's Poorly)' proved popular with the audience, as did 'I Ate Your Da, Don't Judge Me' with its refrain of 'I put the fam in famine, don't put the damn in damning'.

Several historical inaccuracies aside (I'm pretty sure there was no vaping in 1845), this was an impressive directorial debut for Donal Boots, who shot to amateur theatrical fame last year with his homoerotic revival of John B. Keane's *Lent*.

Credit must also be given to Catherine Browne in the lead role, whose wonderful alto voice and ability to devour two pounds of raw offal every night would put Meryl Streep to shame.

Those of you lucky enough to get front-row tickets should bring a raincoat, especially during the Cannibal Céilí towards the end. Recommended!

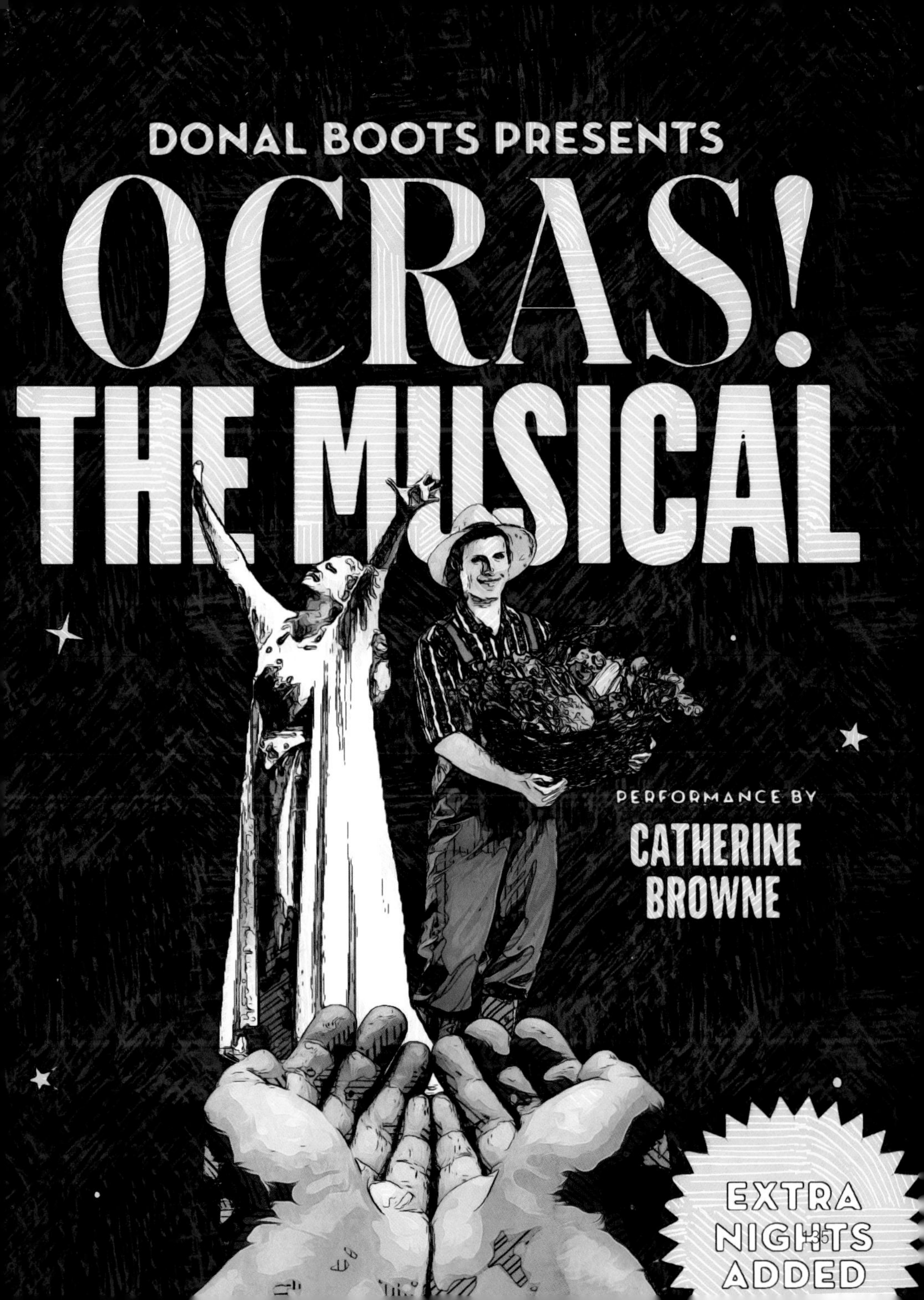
DONAL BOOTS PRESENTS
OCRAS!
THE MUSICAL
PERFORMANCE BY
CATHERINE BROWNE
EXTRA NIGHTS ADDED

THEATRE REVIEW:

The Final Temptation of Brigid

Biographical erotic drama that won't leave you a little cross

BY FÉILIM COURTNEY

LOCAL playwright Sorcha Flanagan Roche delivers a masterpiece in Sapphic historical fiction with her portrayal of the final ten years of the life of Brigid, patron saint of bees and dyslexic-cross makers.

Her best days behind her, Brigid is suffering a crisis of confidence after long ago having offered her virginity to God only for him to holy ghost her. Called Frigid Brigid by her fellow nuns, she is lonely, unfulfilled and questioning her beliefs. Soon, she begins to question much more when her eye is drawn to the amorous Patricia, a new novitiate and former camogie player.

Helen Finnegan gives a passionate performance as the titular saint, and the frequent nudity the role requires shows the benefits of the weekly Zumba classes she teaches in St Patrick's national school. Ms Flanagan Roche is a better writer than actor, but she pursues the role of Patricia with vigour, especially during the 'scribing lesson' scene. I for one will never look at a quill the same way again.

This is a tender and moving drama, despite the inferred relationship between Brigid and Joan of Arc being historically impossible due to the 900-year age gap.

Tickets are completely sold out, so if you are one of the lucky ones, enjoy. If not, I understand there will be a DVD release very soon. For further details contact Derek in the parish centre.

Mary Kennedy in record wicker man escape

TIDY Towns Viagra and self-styled David Attenborough for culchies Mary Kennedy celebrated her hundredth escape from a wicker man yesterday.

Speaking exclusively to *Mallow News* from her chic Dublin home, Ms Kennedy was in jubilant yet typically modest form.

'Well, at this stage, it's quite easy to be honest,' she said. 'It follows an established pattern. I get an invitation from a small town to come and film their harvest celebrations. We arrive, everything seems normal … we look at local initiatives, try the food, pretend to be interested while dying a little inside. Next thing you know, everyone's dancing in the nip, wearing animal masks and trying to stuff me into yet another wicker man to appease a harvest god and guarantee a successful crop. Textbook stuff really.'

'Weren't you scared?'

'Not for myself. I keep a set of lock picks in my bra and make my way out the back door before the flames get near me. It's the cameramen I feel sorry for. They usually end up eviscerated, stuffed with nectar and nailed to a beehive. I've lost five so far this year. Danny, on this last one, was tied to a maypole and slowly crushed to death while Jack L sang "Georgie Boy" from the back of a lorry.'

'What keeps you going?'

'Ah sure look it's a bit of craic and it's a great opportunity to put the spotlight on small businesses. Making wicker men is a dying art. Although I would occasionally like to be imprisoned in a wicker woman,' she laughed.

Good woman, Mary. We'll see you in Doneraile this June for Solstice Slaughter 2020.

Bertie Ahern to broker peace deal between Dickie Rock and Johnny Logan

ARCHITECT of the Good Friday Agreement and occasional cupboard dweller Bertie Ahern was yesterday appointed chief mediator in the long-running feud between elderly music icons Richard 'Dickie' Rock and Johnny 'Johnny' Logan.

The feud was sparked when Mr Logan 'dissed' Mr Rock in an interview with the *Irish Times*, a paper for Dubliners who like rugby and white neighbours. Specifically, Mr Logan accused Dickie of living in a fantasy world, which Mr Rock strongly refuted, stating, 'I only return to Narnia when the great Aslan summons me.'

The former showband sensation then escalated matters by saying he would give Johnny Logan a 'fucking box' to which the Eurovision winner responded, 'I love sex boxes.'

When it was explained that he was being threatened with violence, Mr Logan asked for a mediator to be appointed to broker peace, as 'My face is my passport. I can't travel without it.'

Luckily, the former Taoiseach and banking novice was able to intervene.

'My first question was "How much does this pay?"' Mr Ahern told reporters from his Drumcondra home. 'When the answer was nothing, I said no. Then, when I realised it would keep my name in the papers, I relented. I mean, Michael D. Higgins can't live forever, can he? No, really, can he? Because I've heard the rumours.'

Formal mediation will begin next week in the Powerscourt Hotel at Mr Ahern's insistence, as 'the water pressure in the showers is A1'.

CULTURE NIGHT
Your guide to the best events in and around Ireland

ESTABLISHED in 2006 to allow common, decent people the opportunity to poke around gaffs they'd normally be thrown out of, Culture Night is an annual celebration of the arts and is in no way a desperate attempt to justify the receipt of government grants. This is just a taste of what's on offer.

Cork City

As Culture Night gives the public access to properties normally closed to them, for one night only, Cork people in their twenties will be allowed access to affordable housing.

Dublin

The Georgian Society are delighted to allow members of the public limited access to Twink. Please remember to bring a crucifix! Make sure to pop into the city's famous Live Museum of Homeless People. This interactive attraction shows no sign of closing.

Galway

This year's theme is 'self-satisfaction'. See the fairy fort where Michael D. Higgins was born or maybe watch the locals navigate roundabout after roundabout in an act of interminable Sisyphean torture.

Kerry

The kind folk at Weyland-Yutani will be throwing open their doors to the public for the first time ever. See the labs where the Healy-Raes are created. Look at the vats containing the less successful versions of Fungie. A must-see for all the family.

Kilkenny

The city's GAA hall of fame throws open its doors to show its famous 200-year-old bogman or, as he's known locally, 'Brian Cody'.

Limerick

There is a book-burning in the city library at 8p.m., feel free to bring your own lighter fuel. This year's theme is evolution.

Roscommon

A night of protesting immigrant rights will take place across the county outside direct provision centres. Bring your hoods.

Waterford

Check out 'Blaasé', the newest exhibition in the city's Heritage Museum, celebrating the driest bread known to man. Did you know: blaas were used by the Germans to construct dams during the Second World War?

Marty Whelan escapes RTÉ

AN INVESTIGATION is underway after infamous Montrose lifer Marty Whelan escaped from custody while presenting his radio show on Lyric FM.

Suspicions were raised when his studio was found empty during morning roll call. A subsequent search revealed an escape tunnel hidden behind a well-worn poster of Nanci Griffith.

CCTV footage released by gardaí shows the prisoner nimbly hopping through the minefield used to contain the cast of *Fair City*, over the Craig Doyle clone mass grave and finally emerging naked from a sewer pipe, covered in faeces and howling in the rain.

'This is particularly disturbing,' said Detective Frank Toner, 'as he could just have gone out the fire exit.'

Director General Dee Forbes made an emotional plea for Mr Whelan to return, saying he was 'one of the cheaper ones'. She added, 'Honestly, I've been leaving Tubridy's cell open for months and he hasn't taken the bait.'

This is the second such escape this year. *Today* presenter Dáithí Ó Sé successfully chewed through his restraints in February. He was captured hours later at the Red Cow Luas stop, trying to hitchhike west. Luckily for him doctors were able to reattach his hand.

Ms Forbes has said Mr Whelan's whereabouts are currently 'unknown' but that gardaí are pursuing a definite line of enquiry following the discovery of a postcard from Mark Cagney inviting Mr Whelan to join him across the border in Ballycastle.

Stars in focus, with Larry Egan:

KIM JONG-UN

KIM JONG-UN was having his usual Friday night in with the lads. The 'bad boy' of international politics was eating a bowl of burger meat when a sharp pain shot through his left arm and he broke out in a sweat. The Spear of Pyongyang, Great Stallion of Korea and Karaoke Queen of Lillie's was having a heart attack.

'It was a wake-up call for me, to be honest, Larry,' he tells me over a smooth Zoom call a week later. 'I was treating my body like a treacherous uncle, strapping it to a cannon and shooting it into space. Metaphorically speaking, of course.'

Looking sharp in his trademark suit and dynamic fade haircut, he seems to be the picture of health – but nothing could be further from the truth.

'It was touch and go for a while,' he admits. 'I had my cardiologists executed every time they suggested diet or exercise so, when it came time for my surgery, I had to use the state veterinarian. He replaced my heart with that of a mighty stag.'

So, it's a case of Deer Leader, then. Did he have the vet killed too?

'Well, you know me, Larry. Executions are my Pringles. Once you pop, eh?'

They say a brush with death can change you profoundly.

'Oh absolutely. I'm ashamed to say I was a workaholic, but I'm trying to delegate more now. I've handed over management of the nuclear programme to my sister and outsourced propaganda to the BBC.'

And what about his love life? I remember how on our many nights out in Dublin he always had some young one on his arm.

'Love is like a missile,' he says, uncharacteristically sombre for a moment. 'You think it's going to hit America but it goes hopelessly off course. But I'm an optimist, I'll always keep trying.'

And, as for the rumours about him and Roz Lipsett … I tell him they always seemed like love's young dream.

He smiles slyly. 'No comment.'

Nathan Carter goes to hell

Dimensional portal claims soul of bizarrely popular singer

THERE were terrifying scenes at a Nathan Carter concert last Saturday night, when the ten-thousandth performance of 'Wagon Wheel' resulted in a portal to hell opening in the floor of the Majestic Ballroom, *Mallow News* reports. Mr Carter, a Liverpudlian Ken doll with the charisma of Ted Bundy, was halfway through the first verse of his 'signature tune' when things turned sinister and the air begin to shimmer then rip, like cloth.

'I heard an unearthly shriek,' said barman and eyewitness Karl Fortune. 'At first, I thought it was yer man's singing, but then a large vortex appeared in the dance floor, filling the room with a mixture of sulphur and incense. Then these … creatures appeared. They pounced on members of the audience, ripping them apart midair and feasting upon them. It was total chaos. One of the older barmen said he hadn't seen anything like it since Joe Dolan's day.'

He passed out soon after, but not before hearing what he claims was an 'unearthly' voice calling Mr Carter's name.

Video footage retrieved from a concert-goer's mobile phone shows Mr Carter emerging from the eviscerated remains of his drummer Large Al McGovern and stammering, 'Here, my lord. I hide from thee no more.'

A large, lidless eye then seems to appear in the centre of the dimensional gateway, appraising the singer with a cold, calculating detachment. Transcript as follows:

Unidentified Voice: HAVE YOU NOT HAD FAME?

Carter: I have, my lord.

Unidentified Voice: HAVE YOU NOT HAD FORTUNE?

Carter: I have, my lord.

Unidentified Voice: DESPITE NO DISCERNIBLE TALENT.

Carter: Well … I …

Unidentified Voice: THAT WASN'T A QUESTION.

Carter: Please, I just need more time.

Unidentified Voice: YOU'LL HAVE TIME ENOUGH IN HELL. THE CONTRACT IS FULFILLED.

The footage ends abruptly.

One fortunate fan, who had just returned from the men's toilets, claims Mr Carter simply 'melted away, like an ice-cream in the sun'.

Other survivors corroborated this version of events, declining offers of a partial refund. 'Fair play to Nathan,' said one fan, 'he knows how to put on one hell of a show.' The ballroom will be closed for renovations and a routine exorcism, meaning next week's Coronas gig will now be cancelled, providing the town with some much-needed respite.

RTÉ launches exciting new autumn schedule

THE stars were out in force at Montrose yesterday to launch RTÉ's dynamic new autumn schedule. Smiling desperately, the cream of Ireland's talent pool gathered around Director General Dee Forbes as she gave television-licence holders yet another reason to break the law. Here is just a small selection of what's to come:

Better Call Shawl:

Amy Huberman stars in a new drama that asks: What would happen if Peig Sayers was a crooked solicitor working for the IRA?

Say Yes to Redress:

Sisters of Charity are pursued around a giant maze until they finally pay the fucking money they owe victims of child abuse.

Heaney in a Bottle:

Poetry and alcohol? What could possibly go wrong in this talent show that pits Ireland's rhymers against each other while getting blind drunk.

Heavy Petting:

Celebrity vet Karl Madden helps treat pets suffering from morbid obesity. Will spaniel FooFoo survive another round of liposuction? Does miniature pony Lilo have Type 2 diabetes? Find out this October.

Vocation, Vocation, Vocation:

This new reality show follows three trainee priests as they navigate their way through seminary school. You'll fall in love with Pádraig, Simon and Ronan as they laugh, pray and attempt to stay on the straight and narrow during a pilgrimage to Rome. Narrated by Amy Huberman.

Hang the PJ:

Funny man and radio presenter P.J. Gallagher tries to avoid being lynched by members of the general public. Marty Whelan hosts this fun new gameshow from the makers of *The Purge*. Amy Huberman also stars.

Mock the Weak:

Ireland's finest comedians face their toughest audience yet: residents at Coolmount Hospice.

Where in the World is Aidan Gillen?

A quiz show starring actor Aidan Gillen as he improvises scenes and contestants try to figure out where the fuck his characters are supposed to be from.

Do Not Resuscitate:

Amy Huberman stars as a high-flying surgeon who tries to balance a successful career with her turbulent personal life. Also starring Liam Cunningham as Professor Frank Socialist, her mentor and married lover. From the makers of all the other shit she's been in.

Are You More Smarty Than A Marty?

Primary-school children pit their wits against Martys Morrissey and Whelan in a family quiz show from the makers of *The Chase*.

Bishop Takes King:

Des Bishop and Ciara King star in this new travel show that takes in the sights and sounds of rural Ireland. Watch Des show Ciara his 'hidden' Ireland while also performing his new stand-up show. Expect plenty of humour as Des shares what he finds so funny about the Irish despite living here for 30 fucking years.

Dustin the Turkey murdered by Niall Horan fans

IRELAND'S celebrity community was in mourning last night as the body of popular entertainer and former presidential candidate Dustin The Turkey was discovered in an abandoned Dublin city centre apartment, *Mallow News* reports.

The unmistakable aroma of Christmas dinner wafted through Fairview as the Dublin icon's roasted remains were removed from the scene by the state pathologist's office, while members of the gardaí sobbed and made gravy.

Dustin was reported missing by his partner, former *Love Island* contestant Maura Higgins, three days ago, sparking a nationwide search that sadly culminated in last night's gruesome discovery of his mutilated body in a catering oven.

Mr The Turkey had participated in RTE's *Comic Relief* on Friday night, reuniting with his fellow puppets Zig, Zag and Ray D'Arcy in a tribute to their old TV show *The Den*.

Former One Direction star Niall Horan made a brief appearance, in which he was mildly ridiculed by Dustin before being cut off while about to play one of his hits.

This did not go down well with Mr Horan's teenage cult following, who felt that the treatment of the Mullingar moppet was 'disrespectful' and 'shameful', even though the perpetrator was, you know, a fucking puppet.

The online fury culminated in an anonymous post on RTÉ's Facebook page on Saturday that simply read, 'You roasted Niall. Now we will roast you.'

Dustin disappeared soon after.

Speaking from an undisclosed location and currently under the state's witness protection programme, Ray D'Arcy told *Mallow News* of his sadness at the loss of his long-time associate.

'Dustin was one of the greatest entertainers and lovers this country has ever known. He was more than just a bird with a hand up its anus. He was my friend.'

The Eurovision star's funeral will take place at the Pro-Cathedral next Sunday, with former president Mary McAleese acting as guest celebrant. He will be interred in a bin outside Supermac's afterwards.

If you have any information that may be of value or know a decent recipe for stuffing, please contact Clontarf garda station.

Five ways to turn your uncommunicative, GAA-loving husband into an uncommunicative, GAA-loving

CONNELL

THE television show *Normal People* has taken the country by storm this past month, with its frank and honest portrayal of young love in twenty-first-century Ireland. Set in an alternative universe where people from Sligo are attractive, the show focuses on the on/off relationship between shy and sensitive Marianne and shy and sensitive Connell as they navigate school, university and classism while engaging in athletic bouts of lovemaking that would make a statue move, and not in the way the locals in Ballinspittle would be used to.

Arguably the star of the show, Paul Mescal has brought more moisture to Ireland than the Beast from the East. Today, we show you the top five ways to turn your own uncommunicative, sports-loving partner into an … eh … uncommunicative and GAA-loving Connell.

1 **The chain:** A miraculous medal is a key part of the look. If you can't convince your partner to wear one, try shaving his chest hair into the shape of a scapular while he sleeps.

2 **Brooding:** One of the keys to Connell's sexual magnetism is a far-off stare that communicates more than words or writing could ever say. To replicate that look of thoughtful intensity in your partner, simply ask him who would win in a fight between Lionel Messi and Ronaldo.

3 **Lovemaking:** Connell is in his early twenties, the sexual peak of any man's life. More likely than not, your partner finishes faster than Usain Bolt. Introduce a competitive element by having Ger Canning commentate during intercourse. This is a service he provides for free, apparently, so what have you got to lose?

4 **Sensitivity:** Connell feels secure enough in his relationship to discuss his feelings with Marianne. Your husband would rather be waterboarded than let you know what he wants for dinner. We suggest micro-dosing him with MDMA. Pretty soon he'll be telling you how he feels while licking every lightbulb in the house.

5 **O'Neill's shorts:** No Irish woman can resist the sight of a man's milky-white flesh chafing erotically against the taut microfibres of a pair of O'Neill's shorts. Watch and marvel at your man as he cavorts around your love chamber, perspiration neatly contained by the shorts' in-built sweat-wicking system.

Follow our advice and, pretty soon, your other half will be a new person. Or, alternatively, just find someone else. I mean, whatever's easier.

The Coronas not confirmed for Mallow Arts Festival

MUSIC fans were singing for joy this morning when Irish band The Coronas were confirmed not to be playing this year's arts festival. Director of Events Tadhg Foley has said they will not be playing Friday, Saturday or Sunday of the May bank holiday weekend.

'When you organise an annual arts festival, the danger is you run out of acts not to include,' he said. 'So I'm really pleased we've managed to go another year without having these ear molesters haunting the brains of our town like auto-tuned ghosts.'

Formed in hell, The Coronas are what would happen if you tied mediocrity to a chair, beat it with a sock filled with an Oasis songbook and then forced it into the pale body of an agricultural science student who thinks facial hair and a sul-

len expression are a fitting substitute for charisma or talent.

A permanent fixture on the Irish music scene for what feels like millennia, they have sound-tracked the bland, joyless sex lives of couples who work in HR and occasionally the birthing of yet another future chartered accountant.

This non-appearance marks the first time The Coronas have not played an Irish festival.

When asked if there were any other surprises in store, Mr Foley added, 'We're not in talks with Ham Sandwich and Jack L, but it's only February. I've got a feeling 2020 is going to be a great year for Irish music.'

Tickets for Mallow Arts Festival can be purchased in local shops or online at TicketBastard.

Ask Danny

Dáil bad boy and squeeze-box lover Danny Healy-Rae is renowned for his university-of-life, hedge-school-of-hard-knocks attitude. Now, he writes exclusively for *Mallow News* as Ireland's straightest-talking agony uncle, giving advice on sex, relationships and problems with the occult.

Dear Danny,

I'm a farmer by trade and have been all my life. I have never known the touch of a woman except for that of my dear mother who passed away over the Christmas. I'm tempted to 'get out there', as they say, and find a girl of my own, but I'm not sure I have the experience. What should I do?

Helpless in Kilmallock

Well, Helpless, it's a strange old world to be getting out there as a single man, and that's for certain. The nephews are always telling me about this app and that, but no godless technology can ever take the place of the old ways: getting absolutely paralytic and heading to your local taxi rank or mass rock to find a partner. What woman can resist the Irish male in full flow, shirt half tucked in, tie over his shoulder, shiteing on about the price of silage while trying to hide his erection during the 'Siege of Ennis'. No woman can resist, though if she can, then she's not the woman for you.

As for experience … as a man once said to me, you can't bull a cow without giving him the horn, so make sure and eat proper – meat, veg, gravy, the Kerry five a day. When you find yourself in a romantic situation, nature will take over and as sure as the world's flat, she'll be ating out of your hands like a baby lamb on Easter Sunday, and you can take that to the bank.

Danny

Dear Danny,
I've always had bad luck with my health, and, whenever I see you on the telly, I'm struck at how robust you look. I've tried exercise, giving up meat and even, God help me, the drink, to no avail. Can you tell me your secret?
Curious in Kanturk

Dear Curious,

I tell you this now, and it's the God's honest truth. I have never been sick a day in my life. So-called doctors attribute it to the fact that I was born with three stomachs and an additional four foot of intestine, but that's only nonsense. I eat a pound of raw mince and liver every day, and my bowels have been as regular as the Angelus. So, get that vegetarian nonsense out of your head, it'll only bring you misery, sure didn't a fella up the road try eating vegetables for a week and he left his wife for a builder in Tralee.

As for drink? Did you know drinking two glasses of stout a day reduces your chances of being bitten by a púca? Are you willing to take that chance? I thought not.

I will let you in on a little secret, though … whenever I feel a sniffle or a fit coming on, I go straight to my local fairy fort, stick my arm in the window and wait. Eventually, one of the wee folk will take my hand in theirs and we shake until he spits in my palm for good luck. I then rub my hands together, say a decade of the rosary and go on my way, cured of whatever unholy ailment was trying to take hold of me.

So, if you want to be healthy and happy, throw your modern medicine into the rubbish bin along with your vegan cookbooks and take my advice: eat, drink and be merry and when in doubt, tickle a fairy.

Yours,
Danny

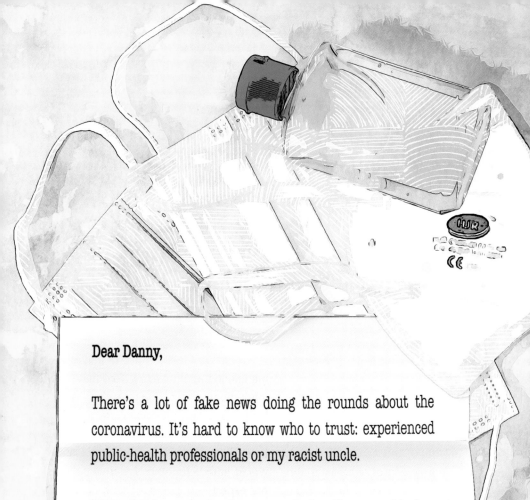

Dear Danny,

There's a lot of fake news doing the rounds about the coronavirus. It's hard to know who to trust: experienced public-health professionals or my racist uncle.

With all this confusion I was wondering if you could clear up where this all started, what's the story with washing my hands and quarantining – and are the army going to kill my grandparents?

Yours sincerely,
Confused in Carrigaline

Well, Confused, you've come to the right man to straighten you out. People can be fierce malicious in these times and it's important to know who to trust. First of all, you're as well off staying in. If you miss the old drop, I'll be doing the rounds in a supertanker for the next few months spraying a mixture of stout and carvery gravy into the open mouths of anyone who wants it. Hit me up on the 'gram if you want to know more.

Regarding hygiene, yerra the HSE must be on drugs. I only wash my hands once a month before leafing through my copy of *Alive!* and I recommend you do the same.

In terms of where it came from, make no mishtake – this is a Chinese virus,

manufactured in the same labs that they made homosexuality back in the sixties. If you're brave enough to keep ating them chicken balls, make sure you rinse them right. That maniac in the Schtates would have you using bleach when every expert knows you need holy water that's been blessed by a priest with no previous convictions.

I can personally assure you that the army are not going to kill anyone as they are too busy completing the Ark I asked them to build as part of my agreeing to the last Programme for Government.

I hope that clears things up for you.

All the best with the virus.
Danny

Literary

CORNER

Exclusive extract from Ordinary Shams 2

CORK author Gillian Mooney rose to prominence in 2015 when she published her second novel *Ordinary Shams*, to international acclaim. The book, which centred on the on/off relationship between GAA handballer Fergus and posh property developer's daughter Caroline, was a publishing sensation, selling 5 million copies. Deliberately open-ended, the author said she would never write a sequel. Five years and one crippling gambling habit later, that sequel has finally arrived. *Mallow News* has an exclusive extract from the first chapter of *Ordinary Shams 2: Ghost Protocol*.

Fergus lifts a tub of mayonnaise and empties it slowly into a dispenser. The Centra has been quiet for the last two hours. So quiet that his manager has left him to lock up. Good. He finishes at the deli counter, picks up his copy of *For Whom the Bell Tolls*, and lets his brow furrow attractively in concentration.

The door opens. Fergus sighs, and puts the paperback down. 'How can I—' He stops.

'I heard you were back.'

He nods, saying nothing, as he still uses a lack of verbosity to hide his inner sensitivity.

'How long?'

He looks at her. Caroline Skeevy-Gilet. She hasn't changed in the last five years. Still plain in a beautiful way. Skin as pale as a frozen *jambon*, hair the golden colour of a Cuisine de France baguette. God, he really needed some time away from the deli counter.

'Three months and change,' he says.

She purses her lips. 'What happened in New York?'

He wants to tell her. How intimidating it was. How having a degree from a college that ranks 165th in the world wasn't the blank cheque he thought it was. How the people on his creative-writing course mocked him for wearing tracksuits to class and drinking milk from a Lucozade bottle. How he's earning more in one week at Centra than a writer could hope to make in a month.

'I don't want to talk about it,' he says. 'What about you, what have you been up to?'

She tells him her father pulled some strings for her in the civil service and she now works as a private secretary for the Minister for Justice.

'That's the handsome one,' he says.

'Yes,' she says. And the married one as well. Fleetingly, she thinks about Michael, the family photo on his desk and how he always places it face down when they have sex.

There is a long silence.

'I don't suppose you want to have a quick ride, for old times' sake,' he says.

She blushes. 'All right, so. Do you still have your chain?'

'No,' he admits. 'But I have a lanyard.'

'That'll do, I suppose,' she says, dragging him into the walk-in freezer.

'I don't suppose I can have a lottery ticket,' says Mrs McGinty.

The noises she hears soon after answer her question for her. *At least one of us is getting lucky*, she thinks.

Vintners' Association launches new PintHub site for lonely drinkers

THE coronavirus lockdown has been difficult on many of our citizens, none more so than that most treasured of Irish stereotypes, the casual alcoholic. Unable to frequent public houses, these poor souls are instead forced to engage with their families, drink at home and urinate carelessly on their own bathroom floors.

Conscious of this, the Vintners' Association today launched a new subscription-only website for lonely drinkers desperate to engage in traditional pub activities. Called PintHub, the site provides subscribers access to exclusive live-streaming content, such as pint-pouring, shite drunk talk and impromptu racism, all for the cost of a pint a week.

The site has already amassed 5,000 subscribers, with the most popular page dedicated to the aforementioned pint-pouring. A barman, identity undisclosed, slowly and provocatively pours a pint of Guinness live online while users leave comments.

'Pubs provide a vital social outlet for many people, especially in rural areas,' said Conor Gowlbag of the VA. 'We hope this new service will help reconnect them and remind them that cheap drink and connecting emotionally with your family is no substitute for a real Irish pub. This is a virtual experience, but we hope it fills the gap, at least until we've successfully lobbied the government to fast track reopenings.'

Horoscopes

WITH TINA PENDRAGON

Blessed at birth with the sight to see beyond the human veil, Tina Pendragon, astrologer and chartered accountant, tells you what your future holds. Remember, this is an exact science as proved recently by scientists at MIT (Mallow Institute of Technology).

Aries

The world is your oyster. Unfortunately, you are allergic to shellfish. Love blooms with a chance encounter at the emergency room.

Gemini

The time has come to take a good look at the man in the mirror. Because he's been standing behind you for an hour now.

Taurus

You find yourself running out of material for a horoscope piece and use a lazy fourth-wall-breaking technique for a cheap laugh.

Cancer

Open your heart to joy. Alternatively, take antidepressants. Basically, just cheer up – you're a bit of a Debbie Downer.

Leo

Beware the green-eyed monster. Sharon in HR hates your guts.

Virgo

He knows, Frank. He unlocked my phone and read our messages. Meet me at 'our' place on Sunday afternoon. Know that I love you.

Libra

You will spend an inordinate amount of time on the toilet reading a local news book that a loved one bought you as an afterthought.

Scorpio

Congratulations! It's your turn to become the new Minister for Agriculture.

Sagittarius

You are the life and soul of the party, a chronic alcoholic. As soon as one door closes, another one opens. Fix your bloody doors, Sharon.

Capricorn

It is time to grow up and realise the vengabus is never going to come for you, never mind the 203 to Farranree.

Aquarius

You will meet an old friend from school you haven't seen in years and quietly revel in how terribly she's aged. You will mention this to your husband, who will mutter something about 'try looking in the shagging mirror'.

Pisces

Time to wash that man right out of your hair. After all, it's DNA evidence that could be used to secure a conviction.

Locals in Profile:
Declan Culain

DECLAN CULAIN may look like an ordinary Irish taxi driver by day – ruddy of cheek, twinkly of eye and casually racist of speech – but, by night, he is Mallow's very own witchfinder. *Mallow News* interviewed Declan in his council office, which he shares with the town's official paedophile.

MN: Declan, first of all, can you tell us, what exactly is a witchfinder?

DC: Well, I want to dispel any myths out there that witches aren't real. They are. They live among us. Many, if not all, are women. And it is my job, part-time, to find them using the tools of my trade and my innate fear of the feminine form.

MN: Fascinating. And when you say tools …?

DC: I have a pair of pliers that date back to the 1950s, that's my truth finder. A scrying crystal that used to belong to Brian Boru, that's my way finder. And an Indigo Girls CD. That's my lure.

MN: And how did you get the job? Was it an interview?

DC: My father was a finder of witches and his father before him. You have to inherit the job, not earn it. This is Ireland, after all.

MN: According to some, we live in more enlightened times. So, do witches even exist anymore?

DC (darkly): We are surrounded by them. Witches take many forms. Homeopaths, influencers, lesbian geography teachers that won't text you back after the first date.

MN: OK. So, tell us, if you can: do you catch many witches?

DC: I do, I do. Book groups, Tupperware parties, the Cauldron pub and sex dungeon outside of Buttevant. Anyone looking to buy foreskin on Done Deal. You need to know all the signs, like … eh … doing their own DIY. I mean, come on! Hello, Satan!

MN: And when you finally catch them?

DC: I utter Our Lord's prayer to bind them to me and, thanks to our town's charter, they are also legally obliged to accompany me to the testing ground for proofing and sentencing.

MN: Proofing and sentencing?

DC: Yes. We require proof. We're not savages. They must pass three scientific trials in order to be declared Not A Witch and get their certificate.

MN: And those trials are?

DC: They must survive 40 dunkings in the dunking pool. (He indicates an inflatable paddling pool in the corner of his office.)

DC: Trial number two, they must survive an hour of being Told To Smile by a patronising man while resisting the overwhelming urge to murder him. Finally, the hardest of trials, they are forced to denounce the Great Beast, Joanne Cantwell.

MN: Joanne Cantwell?

DC (spits): Joanne Cantwell.

MN: And the sentencing?

DC: If guilty they be, the sentence is always the same. They are to be burned at the stake.

MN: Good lord.

DC: Of course, we can't do that anymore, thanks to the feckin' Hague, so I get them to hold a lighted Jo Malone candle and say 'Ouch'.

MN: Thank you, Declan, this has been ... illuminating?

DC: Easy now. This isn't *The New Yorker*, sham.

We leave Declan now, deep in thought and drawing pentagrams onto his desk with the pointy end of a compass. One of Mallow's characters. Until next time, see you all soon. In town, no doubt.

MALLOW THROUGH THE YEARS
The Crash of '79

MOST locals will be aware of the Mexican pilot who crash-landed at Mallow Racecourse in 1983, becoming a local *cause célèbre* and increasing the town's diversity by 100 per cent.

This was actually the second crash of its kind, the first occurring in July 1979 when Colombian pilot Jorgé Castilla made an emergency landing in a field outside Dromahane after his Gulfstream II was shot down by Kevin Duffy, a local hermit who was still unaware the Civil

War had ended and thought Dev was trying to control his thoughts from the air.

Both pilot and plane emerged relatively unscathed from the crash, but several parts had to be ordered from Dublin to repair the engine, meaning Jorgé was at his leisure in the town for a period of time.

The Colombian became quite popular with the locals, especially the ladies, and could be found in the Central Hotel bar every evening regaling them with tales of foreign lands and food that didn't taste of recession.

His enjoyment soon evaporated, however, when he discovered that local gardaí had impounded his cargo, promising to 'mind it' for him until he was ready to go on his way.

As Jorgé spent his days desperately petitioning the guards, Mallow experienced its most productive summer on record, with local farmers reportedly harvesting day and night, and tradi-

Central Hotel

tional musicians creating some of the worst Irish music ever made. Public health records also show a pernicious cold among the populace and a spike in paranoiac episodes.

In mid-August, a carload of Jorgé's business associates arrived from Cartagena via Cork airport anxious to 'catch up' with him. The pilot left soon after, but you could say he left a little piece of himself behind, and not just the fingers Pat Hickey found in the town park a week later.

Just as the Spanish Armada has been blamed for the dark complexion of some Galwegians, so traces of Jorgé Castilla can be seen in the odd adult around the town, who spent many the Father's Day looking at the sky in vain, hoping for the return of their sky dada.

MALLOW THROUGH THE YEARS

Surf's Up: The arrival of broadband in Mallow

IN THE early noughties, if you spoke about 'broadband' to a Mallow man, the first thought that came to mind was 'Are Bananarama playing the Hiland again?'

That was all to change in 2005 when the information superhighway finally arrived in the town.

The internet had previously only been accessible via a dial-up connection in the local library, as rural connectivity was still problematic. Queues would extend down the main street, full of men anxious to catch up on the weekend's sport, women looking for celebrity gossip and teenage boys looking for that side-boob shot of Teasy McDaid from 'Dinny's Wedding Night, the infamous banned episode of *Glenroe.*

At the official launch in the youth centre, town librarian and taxidermist Candide Grainger welcomed the move, as it meant the library could now focus on providing reading material rather than cleaning up after so-called intimacy hours brought in to alleviate the loneliness of the region's farmers.

Locals were delighted that they would now have fast, unlimited access to the internet, as long as they had a tall, athletic child willing to roam the house with the router looking for a strong connection, not unlike a bachelor farmer during intimacy hour.

Parish priest Fr Cannon was the only dissenting voice, comparing the internet with the serpent in the Garden of Eden, tempting Adam and Eve with the promise of unlimited knowledge. We can only assume he had a change of heart as his laptop was seized by the Garda National Cyber Crime Bureau in late 2006.

It is worth noting that the rollout encompassed all areas with the exception of Buttevant, as they had only recently gone electric and it was felt that too much change might cause irreversible psychological trauma.

MALLOW THROUGH THE YEARS
Miss Mallow 1923

IN THE summer of 1923, Mallow was facing a crisis. All of its eligible young women had been lost to mating raids by neighbouring towns, which threatened the annual Miss Mallow competition, a source of much-needed income.

The town council, under the aegis of Mayor Bill 'the Bribe' Daly, had a decision to make – cancel the festival and deal with the economic and emotional fallout or go ahead with a selection of local spinsters.

Instead, they went for something far more radical and decreed that the festival would proceed but with male contestants dressed as women. There were no objections from the church, as homosexuality had yet to be invented.*

Five contestants applied, lured by the winner's prize of 200 John Player Blue and unfettered access to the town condom.

The contest took place in the parish hall and was hosted by local TD Mattie Singleton, who had experience dealing with crowds as he helped organise impromptu hangings of pro-Treaty forces during the Civil War. Much like the Rose of Tralee, each contestant would come on, introduce themselves, have a little banter with the host and then do their party piece.

Cooper Francie Golden came first, castrating a bull while singing 'The Parting Glass'. Jimmy Stone followed, losing a pint of blood trying to shave his legs with a sheep shears. Fishmonger's son Paul O'Brien recited a poem, despite

that not being an actual talent. All were dressed 'hilariously' in gowns they'd borrowed from their mothers. It was good, clean fun.

The trouble started when it came the turn of barber's apprentice Seany Ford.

Dressed like Constance Markievicz in an episode of *Love Island,* Seany took the stage, much to the admiration of a very confused crowd, composed mainly of local farmers high on harvesting and cider.

Seany proceeded to perform a sensual tango with a hurley while listing off the best way to make a carvery, in an unholy display of Irish sensuality. The hall soon erupted in a mass of drunken lust and confusion.

When the gardaí eventually cleared the room, all that was left of Seany was a hairpin and a pair of rubber bosoms. The town council, eager to avoid a scandal, blamed the riot on Protestants, which was practically an Olympic sport in Ireland at the time.

As for young Seany, some locals maintain he was forced into a loveless marriage like every other local woman and spent the rest of his days working on a beet farm outside Mitchelstown. Others say he fled to Dublin and started a successful entertainment career under the stage name 'Twink'.

*As you know, homosexuality was invented in 1965 when Gay Byrne wore a red tie on *The Late Late Show*.

Obituaries

EDDIE HARRINGTON

THE death has occurred at Galilee Hospice of Eddie Harrington, retired meteorologist, at the age of 67.

Born in Tralee, Eddie was famous for being the only Kerryman capable of giving a straight answer to a question. This superpower first manifested itself when he was on the cusp of adolescence.

'I can still remember it to this day,' he told his biographer in 2002. 'My mother had asked me if the dinner was all right and I said it was "adequate". She was aghast.'

'Why didn't you just say, "Well, it is and it isn't", like a normal person?'

'I suppose it never occurred to me that I wouldn't tell people the truth.'

This honesty would prove his undoing when, in 1986, RTÉ News asked him, as he was leaving Fitzgerald Stadium, if he fancied Kerry's chances for the three in a row.

'Without thinking I said, "Of course, yeah. We're the best team out there.

Only a fool would think we can't take Tyrone."'

When the recording aired, the entire county turned against him. Pursued by a mob led by an enraged Pat Spillane, he barely left Kerry alive, taking sanctuary in the only county that would appreciate his honesty and straightforwardness: Cork.

He moved to Mallow, where he qualified as a meteorologist and spent his days on a ham radio providing honest weather reports to Kerry farmers who knew that 'It might rain and it mightn't' wasn't the best information when it came time to making decisions about when to harvest their crops.

When his biography *Never Say Yerra Again* was published it was the first book to be banned in Kerry since John B. Keane's erotic novel *The Hungry Butcher*.

Eddie enjoyed some local celebrity at the time but, despite living a full life in Mallow, would always regret not being able to return to his native county.

'It's a beautiful place. Though, I mean, it's not the most beautiful place in the world, it's important to have perspective,' he told *Mallow News* in 2010.

Go ndéana Dia grásta ar a anam dílis.

Obituaries

FRANK BARROW

FRANK BARROW, aged 68, who died peacefully after an accidental multiple stabbing in a Bangkok brothel, was one of Mallow's best-known nightclub owners and misogynists. His string of clubs transformed the local scene by giving middle-aged men on the cusp of divorce the opportunity to make women other than their wives feel very uncomfortable.

Barrow grew up in Ballyflaw and attended the Christians Brothers, where he excelled at athletics, being the only one in his class to successfully avoid being molested. He left at 16 to pursue a career as a security guard for Derek Fairy and the Straights, one of the most popular groups of the showband era, touring the country for a number of years before becoming disenchanted and returning home to serve a five-year sentence for grievous bodily harm.

On his release, he used all his wits, experience and the chain of local pubs

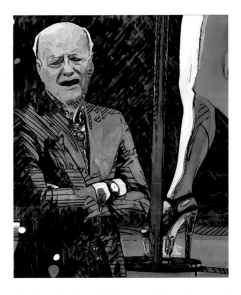

his late father Coleman 'The Bastard' Barrow left him to create his own entertainment empire. He quickly made a name for himself on the live music scene, with luminaries such as Planxty, Thin Lizzy and the Nolan Sisters all refusing to work with him again. In the early eighties, he found his true calling: nightclubs.

Barrow opened Grope! in 1982. Sister venues Fondle and NDA soon followed. Local men loved that they now had an extra two hours to drink themselves into a coma and women loved that the music was so loud, they couldn't hear the shite the men were talking.

But Barrow wasn't just a businessman, he was also an innovator. He invented a vending machine that not only dispensed wedding-ring lubricant but also fake tan to cover the ring line. He even owned several patents such as snack box-flavoured condoms and cigarettes that smelled like Lynx Africa.

Entertainment is a fickle industry, and after a decade or so of success Bar-row's enterprises fell foul of the competition, the problematic economics of nightclubs and being caught illegally filming women in the ladies' toilets. In 1999, he retired in ignominy, leaving his empire to his business partner, Monsignor James Manten.

Later in life, he became enamoured with Buddhism and left Ireland for the Far East to discover himself and avoid the Revenue Commissioners. His final hours were spent surrounded by the things he loved: terrible music, watered-down alcohol and very angry women.

He is sadly missed by his ex-wife Dawn, whose aim was terrible.

Parish notes

Condescension Corner
with Fr Cannon

Greetings, my brothers and sisters,
This week we reflect upon the teachings of the Third Letter of the Corinthians to St Paul, from the Book of Unnecessary Correspondence.

Dear Camelface,

Please stop writing to us. This is borderline harassment. In this instance, love has very much come to an end. We have taken offence and we are very resentful. Take your booming gong and clashing cymbal and shove it up your hoop.

We have started seeing other martyrs (Simon, the Zealot – I think you were in a band together?). He is very handsome and takes the time to visit, instead of bombarding us with preachy letters. We hope you've found happiness with one of your other whores (the Romans are fucking riddled, just so you know). One more word from you and we're getting the law involved.

What the Corinthians are telling us here is that God's love, much like Paul's, is smothering. Even when they are apart, they feel His presence. No matter how infinite the distance, God is always present in our lives. Whether it is when we are at prayer, at work or even when we make our toilet, He is there. God is holy CCTV, with an infinite hard drive that can always be recovered.

The dominion of GDPR holds no sway over His watchful eye. He does not respect your right to be forgotten. Your spiritual fingerprint is forever etched upon His great mind.

As another great prophet once said, 'Every breath you taketh or maketh, yea I shall be watching thee.' Puff Daddy feat. Faith Evans understood the true nature of God even if they were naïve about where Biggie Smalls ended up (hint: it smells like eggs and isn't Buttevant).

All of this is to say that we must always be aware and fearful of God and very, very ashamed of all our works as He sees all, knows all and forgets nothing. Like a woman, only much better.

Just something to remember when you're in the top paddock, tugging at yourself, Paddy Kiely.

Love in prayer,

Fr Cannon

Around the parish

Mallow

• To raise awareness of rural racism there will be a Best of Motown fancy dress competition in the Village Inn on Thursday night, a great chance to see the mayor's Diana Ross impersonation. He's sure to be in the middle of a 'chain reaction'.

• The Lions Club will not be meeting this month after all animals were confiscated by the ISPCA under the Animal Health and Welfare Act.

• Our annual Marty Whelan appreciation festival Marty Grá is next weekend. Tickets are selling fast so make sure to call in to Fiona at the parish centre to secure yours. This year's highlights include Whelan in the Years, a retrospective of Marty's finest work, and You've Lost That Marty Whelan, where Marty lookalikes hide around town and are hunted down by members of the public. Unfortunately, Marty is once again unable to attend due to the restraining order.

• Mallow's Italian Film Festival has been cancelled after it was discovered that none of the selected films had any good nudity in them. Gerry in the Film Club has apologised and has asked if anyone wants to buy a load of hand cream, he'll give them a good price.

• After their defeat to Kerry in the first round of the All-Ireland, the Cork senior football team will be stopping off at Mallow train station just in case you want to throw something at them. Don't worry, they won't fucking catch it.

• *Mallow News* is looking for interns. All you need is enthusiasm, an appreciation of English and a complete ignorance of the rights afforded you under employment law.

Aghinagh

• After last week's reported shortage, an emergency supply of phlegm thankfully arrived on Thursday so that locals could continue to pronounce the town name correctly. Call in to Gary at the council to get your ration, and please bring your own bucket.

• Tickets are still available for our national school's performance of *The Passion of the Christ*. Ms Flynn has put together a touching and interactive interpretation of the Mel Gibson classic. If you're lucky, you might get a chance to scourge Christ himself. Ten euro per adult, senior citizens go free.

• Do you have green fingers? If so, please report to Mallow General for treatment.

Doneraile

• The wi-fi password for Sunday's mass is water2wine. For members of the Communion Club, this month's wafer is strawberry and balsamic vinegar flavour.

• The Cork Union of National Teachers will meet at Barrigan's pub on Sunday at 8p.m. to vote on a new name and acronym.

• Remember, this Saturday marks the annual Purge Night, so motorists are asked to make alternative travel arrangements to avoid unnecessary delays or reapings.

Mourneabbey

• The pungent smell reported last week turned out to be the annual bath night in Clyda.

• Parishioners are advised to stick around after this Sunday's midday mass. Not for any particular reason, the priest's just a bit lonely.

Bweeng

• In an effort to distance themselves from recent controversy surrounding ownership of state hospitals, the Sisters of Charity are to relaunch under the name Birds of Pray. For more info please visit www.bop.ie.

• Our outreach programme for sex-positive seniors, Dogging For Old Dears, has been nominated for the nation's Silver Spaniel Award. Congratulations to Karen and Philip at the Seniors Centre and thanks to Tesco for their discretion.

• Due to the recent good weather, this weekend's mass will be a rerun.

• The Legion of Mary face off against the League of Evil this weekend, so avoid the town entirely – and maybe say a quick prayer for Katie Doolin, who still hasn't recovered her eyesight since her historic battle with Professor Nucleus.

Buttevant

• The annual March Against Science will take place this Friday. This year's theme is Climate Change Is Just God's Farts. Please BYOT (Bring Your Own Torches).

• Great news for local children as the town council has announced a reduction in the working week from 91 to 84 hours. Union head Terry Fortune (7) said he was delighted as he could now spend more time with his wife and children.

• The town will be closed for maintenance all next week so make sure you report to the clinic for your annual scraping.

Dromahane

• Don't forget, this Sunday marks local Father's Day substitute Look, I Was Drunk Day. There will be face-painting at the parish centre and voluntary paternity tests.

• To celebrate annual Culture Night, Dromahane Heritage Club cordially invites you to view the town book. To avoid a repeat of last year's debacle, all crayons are prohibited.

• Hard luck to the boys and girls of St Nathan's secondary school, who failed to qualify for the BT Young Scientist competition with their entry 'Two Legs Good, Three Legs Better'. For next year's competition, it's a toss-up between 'Fire! It Burn Good' and 'If Evolution Is Real, Why Is My Daddy Also My Uncle?'.

• This Friday's Fight Club is cancelled due to an outbreak of foot in mouth at the youth centre.

Lombardstown

• Please show your support for the boys and girls of St Catna's national school in their attempt to break the Guinness world record for the longest human centipede at the youth centre this Sunday afternoon at 2p.m.

• Parishioners should note that because of the recent flu outbreak, the sign of peace will be replaced by that nod men give each other when they've just shared a profound emotional experience but are too repressed to express it.

• Independent TD Dorchas Mathews has organised another blood drive for 15 May. As per local blood transfusion regulations, only virgins can donate and should present themselves to the manor house wearing a simple shift and with the standard NDA completed.

New Twopothouse

• Members of the public are asked to remain vigilant as there have been several reported sightings of Jason Byrne in the New Twopothouse area. Gardaí have asked that you do not approach him or attempt to throw salt at him as that no longer works. Definitely do not engage him in conversation as he will most likely offer to spin straw into gold in exchange for your first-born child. Just call Tom at the station and he'll be out with a crucifix and a bottle of holy water in no time.

• In order to facilitate the triumphant return of our local hurlers at the Old Oak this weekend, we've had to cancel the fundraiser for little Ciara Shanahan. Hopefully there'll still be time for that bone-marrow transplant next month.

Ballyhea

• In local arts news, due to popular demand all future performances of *Blood Brothers* have been cancelled.

• Cumann Eileen, the local Dexy's Midnight Runners Appreciation Society, will hold their AGM at 7p.m. on Thursday, 9 March. New members welcome. Dungarees essential.

Crossword

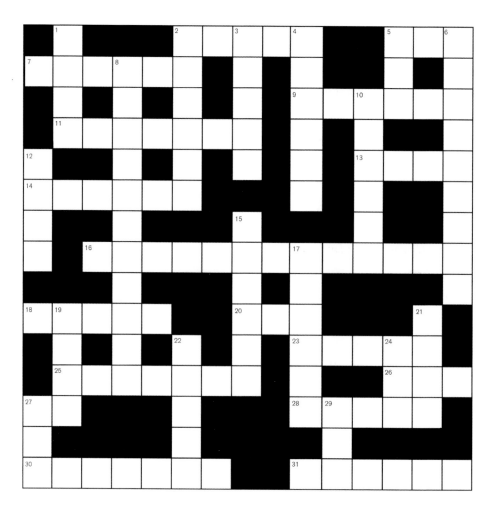

Across

2 (And 1 Down) Would take credit for this clue. (5)

5 Red-breasted creature that nests in Waterford during the summer. (3)

7 Rasputin's official cause of death. (6)

9 Ming, according to Casey. (6)

11 Can be found under the bed of a Blueshirt. (7)

13 Part of Sammy Wilson you might see in the wild. (4)

14 You'd want to be this to vote Fianna Fáil. (6)

16 Anglicised Taoiseach with a smile like a hastily assembled flat pack. (4, 9)

18 Always at it. (5)

20 Number of times a politician has sincerely apologised for a mistake since the foundation of the state. (3)

23 Convicted criminal. (5)

25 As dangerous as three pints. (7)

26 You won't get this in the summer. (3)

27 _____ Boomer. (2)

30 Endangered species in the Dáil. (7)

31 Actor killed by 17 Down. (6)

Down

1 See 2 Across. (4)

2 Famous Dead Zoo in Dublin. (6)

3 See 12 Down. (5)

4 And 21 Down. Hungry (for power) like the wolf. (5)

5 Ulster party that says no to gay cake. (3)

6 Twinned with Chernobyl. (9)

8 If you were the government, I'd be too big to be inside you! (11)

10 And 24 Down. Marty Morrissey was the original one of these. (6)

12 And 3 Down. We came together to do this in 2020. (4)

15 Garth Brooks of poetry for middle-aged men. (6)

17 Venice of north Cork. (6)

19 Beaten by the electorate, not paper or scissors. (4)

21 See 4 Down. (4)

22 When Mayo's curse will be lifted. (5)

24 See 10 Down. (3)

27 Helped 8 Down fit in. (3)

29 Don is drawn to this. (3)

Crossword answers

Across:

2 Shane **5** Dub **7** Coddle **9** Muppet **11** Shinner **13** Arse **14** Tapped **16** Michael Martin **18** Brits **20** Nil **23** Lowry **25** Carvery **26** Tan **27** OK **28** Women **30** Welfare **31** Olivier

Down:

1 Ross **2** Seanad **3** Apart **4** Eamon **5** DUP **6** Buttevant **8** Dáil printer **10** Player **12** Stay **15** Heaney **17** Mallow **19** Rock **21** Ryan **22** Never **24** RTE **27** OPW **29** Owl

Picture credits

The following credits are for images used as the basis for cover and interior illustrations.

Cover images

PA Images/Niall Carson (Phil Hogan, John Delaney); Rollingnews.ie (Danny Healy-Rae); Inpho/Gary Carr (Pat Horgan)

Internal images

PA Images: 27/Brian Lawless; 29/Doug Peters/ Empics Entertainment (Daniel O'Donnell face); 45/ Brian Lawless(Shane Ross face); 47, 53, 55, 61,103/ Caroline Quinn/Damien Eagers/Leon Farrell (Leo Varadkar, Micháel Martin and Eamon Ryan); 71/Yui Mok (Mrs Brown); 73/Niall Carson (Phil Hogan face); 77/ Liam McBurney (Sammy Wilson head and shoulders); 105/Brian Lawless (Luke Ming Flanagan face); 119/Niall Carson/PA Images; 141/Lynne Cameron (Johnny Logan)

Thanks to Pixabay for stock images